THE ADVANTAGE FACTOR

12 Things That Every Aspiring
Young Professional Should Know

Mike A. Williams

THE ADVANTAGE FACTOR

12 Things That Every Aspiring Young Professional Should Know

Mike A. Williams

The Advantage Factor

Cataloging-in-Publication Data is on file with the Library of Congress

ISBN-13: 978-1942140009
ISBN-10: 1942140002

Published by:

Thinknext LLC
3324 Peachtree Rd. NE, Suite 2319
Atlanta, GA 30326

Email: info@mikeawilliams.com
Website: http://www.mikeawilliams.com

PRINTED IN THE UNITED STATES OF AMERICA

This book is dedicated to

My little big girl, my daughter Mikayla. Words cannot express how much daddy loves you and how much joy you have brought into my life. You will always be my greatest achievement—there is no moment in my life where I felt prouder than the day you were born. You are the reason I strive to "Be better and do better" every day.

Table of Contents

PREFACE

In each of our lifetimes, we all reach a pivotal moment where we learn something that will have a lasting impact on our professional and personal lives. Those lessons may be about taking on a new job, building a new home, increasing your education, or just realizing we may not be where we want to be in our careers.

This book is about sharing the lessons I have learned that were instrumental in my professional career and to a lesser degree, my personal life. The intent of this book is to educate and help aspiring young professionals deal with the realities of Corporate America, all the while positioning themselves ahead of their peers to take on more responsibility and advance to the next phase of their profession.

The book includes twelve short lessons focused on mentoring, personal development, networking, leadership, goal-setting, customer satisfaction, adapting, self-awareness, and development. The lessons in this book are structured to be short and serve as a reference you can repeatedly use.

The lessons will include actual examples and stories from my experiences to help drive the point home and, hopefully, provide relevance to something you may be experiencing yourself.

Throughout the book you will find quotes from various leaders and authors that relate to the respective lesson.

Additionally, the lessons will allow you to re-evaluate yourself in relation to your interactions with customers, managers, peers, subordinates, and friends. You will evaluate your weaknesses and adjust your actions to strengthen them. I still have weaknesses of my own, so don't be disappointed if you lack strength in certain areas or if it takes longer to reap the benefits of certain lessons covered in this book. No one will ever be perfect! I certainly am not; growing and learning is a continuous activity.

Don't ever be fooled by writers, or people in general, who try to lead you to believe they have done everything right; that just isn't credible. I always say, "Failing is just one step closer to achievement." You can't achieve anything without failing first. Few people can try something new and be the best at it overnight; so don't get discouraged if you fail early in your career. You have to be constructively dissatisfied in your pursuit of professional and personal growth.

After reading this book, it is my hope that you will be able to apply the lessons to help progress your career and gain some level of success—based on your own definition of what that is to you. I further hope you use the book as a reference for yourself and for others like you—an ambitious young professional looking to advance their career.

ACKNOWLEDGMENTS

Although I invested a lot of time and effort conceptualizing and writing this book, I had a lot of help and support to complete this project. Without the unwavering support, knowledge, and encouragement of so many people, I could not have written this book.

Michelle, thank you for giving me the greatest gift ever. My life would not have the joy it has today without you. Thanks for being a terrific mother, supportive partner, and friend. I will always love you.

To my parents, Barbara and Arthur Wadley, before everyone else, you were my first teachers, coaches, and mentors—everything I am began with your guidance. I love you both dearly.

To my siblings Michelle, Romana, and Torrance, I love you. Thanks for always being there for me.

To my family, friends, past and present co-workers, managers, community leaders, organizations, corporations, mentors, and mentees. Thank you for allowing me to learn something from each of you. I could not write this book without the many lessons and experiences I have accumulated over the years through my interactions and experiences with all of you.

Introduction

Over the years, my knowledge and leadership capabilities have grown due to the wonderful people I have had the privilege of meeting throughout my career. Whether they were co-workers, managers, or other professionals outside of my place of employment, I have grown with the help of so many people. My work as a mentor to so many aspiring young professionals has contributed immensely to my growth and my ability to lead and grow.

Ultimately, some of the primary enablers of my career have been lessons I've learned through first-hand experience. They sometimes say you have to go through it to know it; I learned the hard way about harsh, but appropriate, realities of being an employee. I quickly realized that, while I was important to the success of my organization, as all employees are, I was not the most important person in the company. Leaders of companies often tell employees they are the most important people in the company; and although that is true, as an employee you must put that in the context of the larger picture. Look at it this way—companies are started by shareholders and investors and for a company to stay afloat it has to make money through paying customers; employees cannot be employed or paid without the previous two occurrences. So for me, I always acknowledge that I am important; but at best I will always be number three. I recognize the company needs investors and customers long before it will need me. Since we all like to get paid, we shouldn't expect the pecking order to be any other way.

I also had to face the reality that my personal aspirations would never trump the priorities and well-being of any company I worked for. I learned that, if you dedicate yourself and work hard, the right company, and its management, will recognize your efforts and provide opportunities for you.

In the early years of my career, it became clear that, in order to make an opportunity for myself, I had to teach others and share my knowledge. Additionally, I had to adapt to the ever-changing dynamics of Corporate America and work with a diverse set of people while understanding how their skills, attitudes, and work habits could either be an enabler to my success or a hindrance.

My professional career has taught me the relevance of networking and building relationships with co-workers, management, and people in general, as well as with peers across multiple industry verticals. I have acquired the skills to move beyond my comfort zone both professionally and personally and constantly challenge myself. When I was not being challenged, I was not interested, no matter how much money the job paid. That is still true today.

I found I have a passion for service, for leading and developing others. Sometimes, I fell short delivering on my promise of service, but I have learned to grow with every experience and become better at what I love to do: providing excellent service.

After seventeen years in my chosen profession, I experienced the most pivotal moment in my career, the moment I call the "turning point." It became the basis for Chapter 09: "Know when your time has come." The turning point is a time in your career where you recognize you aren't growing, your opportunities are diminishing, and, most importantly, you aren't happy with what you are doing. My turning point came in 2006 when I left the employer who gave me my first IT job. I admit that, at the time, it was one of the hardest decisions I ever had to make. I felt a variety of mixed emotions. I was afraid, nervous, excited, and anxious all at the same time. But I drummed up enough courage to make a change.

It has been one of the most personally rewarding decisions I ever made. I didn't leave because the company I worked for was a bad company. In fact, I was leaving a great company, which is why I was so afraid and nervous about the decision. I didn't want to make a mistake. As I have often heard, it's easy to know what you have, but you never know what you will be getting into. Nonetheless, at that time I needed a change. I needed to be challenged, so I moved beyond the comfort zone of my first employer. I needed to know I could succeed without the comfort of the seventeen years of legacy and all the relationships I had developed over the years. It was about challenging myself and taking a risk.

I am certain that, during your career, you will come across many things I cover in this book. It is my hope that this book will give you an advantage when facing the same learning curves, challenges and decision-making moments early in your career. Like tennis, when you have the advantage, you are closer than your opponent to winning the round; you always want to be ahead of your competition. By reading this book, I hope you will have the Advantage Factor over your peers!

CHAPTER ONE

Find a mentor to find out who you are

If you have made any positive progression in your life, either personally or professionally, it's safe to say you've made it with some help. That help came in the form of your parents, uncles, aunts, grandparents, siblings, friends, managers, co-workers, or others. On a personal level along your developmental journey, you were given guidance, advice, coaching, encouragement, and support by a select group of family members and friends. Professionally, you have likely found the same aspects in select individuals at work or within professional organizations and associations. These people are your mentors.

Having the right mentor(s) is critical to your personal and professional development—you simply can't succeed without one! With that being said, it should be no surprise I'm beginning with this topic.

Who is a Mentor?

Merriam-Webster defines a mentor as someone who is "a trusted counselor or guide; someone who teaches or gives help and advice to less experienced and often younger persons." In other words, a mentor is someone whose knowledge and experience is both respected and valued. Sometimes people, both young and old, align age and time spent in a particular profession as experience. The assumption is that an older person will always have more knowledge and experience. I disagree that this is always the case. I think my grandmother was right every time she said, "There are some old fools too!" Not everyone who is older will have the right experience and knowledge you require no matter what their age. Many can be classified as a mentor but not everyone will be good at it.

You should know, a mentor does not need to be a senior ranking person within your organization or field. A mentor depends solely on the knowledge and expertise they have to offer in the area and their willingness to advise and guide others with that experience. What you hope to gain determines the right fit for both you and the prospective mentor.

The value of having a mentor

In any field, having a mentor can help you develop and advance your career. A strong mentoring relationship will be built on collaboration, trust, and a mutual commitment by both parties. Some mentorships can happen by chance with no official agreement or acknowledgment of such a relationship.

My first mentor didn't happen by chance. I wouldn't say it was an official mentor and mentee relationship either. My second mentor was destined to be my mentor whether he knew it or not; he was the person I aspired to be. He was well respected and 'knew his stuff'! When he talked, people listened. Both of my first two mentors were passionate about helping me expand my knowledge in a diverse set of areas, and they did it with the intent of teaching me how to lead. In fact, they were more to me than just mentors. They were what I referred to as Knowledge Leaders. I define a Knowledge Leader as *a leader who has experienced both failure and success while acquiring and developing the necessary knowledge, skills, and passion for teaching others how to lead.* I feel mentoring must be done with the intent of teaching others how to lead.

Passion for teaching others is what differentiates Knowledge Leaders from mentors. Not everyone can be a Knowledge Leader, but many qualified leaders can be classified as mentors. With passion, it is not only a leader's desire, it is their duty to teach others to lead as well. In being Knowledge Leaders, my first two mentors had the biggest impact on me during the most critical periods in my young professional career.

I said my "young professional career" because I am of the belief that the most critical time for any individual, professionally or personally, happens between the ages of 22 and 30. It's during this time that you begin to make serious adult decisions about your life. You may complete college, begin your career, begin living on your own, and meet new friends. Once you've done all of that, the real fun starts: you pay real bills! These are the experimental and defining years. You begin to find out who you are and what you really want to be when you grow up. I call those between the ages of 22 and 30 the Aspiring Young Professional (AYP) group of future leaders.

During these years, you learn a lot about yourself. Professionally, you find out if you can lead, adapt, overcome adversity and build relationships. You also learn whether you are a team player or just a hindrance to the team. Personally, you will start thinking about building a family, saving money, buying a car and a house, or making other major decisions. I am also of the belief that the core of who you are and your long-term career trajectory will be determined during this period as well. By the time this period is drawing to an end, you will have experienced many life-defining activities and decisions. You will know who you are and what you want to accomplish. You may make adjustments beyond these years—growth and adapting are natural, and you should always continue to grow, but by age 30 the core of who you are will have already been determined.

It is also critical to find a mentor during these years. These are the years you will need the experience, knowledge, and guidance of respected and admired leaders most; remember, you are defining the core of who you are for the rest of your life. Seek and align with leaders who will give you the best chance of growing and succeeding in both the short and long-term.

The first mentor

I met my first mentor in 1988 while working for my first employer, a leading transportation and logistics company. I had just become a full-time employee after working part-time for a year. We called him Ed Z. He was friendly, outgoing, and the epitome of professionalism. He stood about 6'4" and was one of the few people I had to look up to—literally. At the time, Ed Z. was the equivalent of a Senior Director of Information Technology. In the early days, Ed Z. and I often talked even though I was several levels below him. Ed Z. didn't see titles; he saw people. He was highly effective at managing upwards and downwards. Ed Z. possessed the three Cs of good leadership: Command, Composure, and Communication. He commanded respect when he walked into a room, was always composed no matter the situation, and verbally expressed himself effectively at every level. He treated everyone with respect and fairness. He had an open door policy, one of which I took full advantage—I don't know if it was a good or bad thing for him, but it was great for me. He and I often talked about several topics: work, life, sports, and a host of other things. Ed Z. was a great listener and provided good guidance and advice. He was full of wisdom.

Our relationship didn't begin as a mentor/mentee relationship; it grew into one. In any typical mentoring relationship one participant has more experience, skill, and knowledge than the other; Ed Z. was all of that for me. When I first met him I was young, ambitious and, at 18 years of age, I already thought I knew everything about everything. At least, I thought so until I met Ed Z. He educated me swiftly, but subtly. He taught me that, at my age, I knew very little. I quickly learned he was right; I didn't know anything! He also made me realize I had a bright future ahead of me and larger opportunities were available for me if I remained focused and worked hard. Through Ed Z.'s guidance, support, and constructive feedback for over seventeen years of my early career, I was able to recognize my potential. I found out who I was professionally and what I needed to grow personally. Another crucial lesson Ed Z. imparted was never to burn bridges, because you never knew when you may work for that same person again. I worked for Ed Z. multiple times, directly and indirectly, proving he was right, yet again—it's a small world out there!

As our relationship grew, Ed Z. moved beyond being my mentor to being my *Knowledge Leader*. He wasn't interested in just helping me grow in my current job or in preparing me for the next one; he was always mentoring with the intent and passion of teaching me to lead, no matter what role I held.

Lessons from my mentor

Ed Z. taught me many lessons, some hard, but more useful and understandable as my career progressed. Three primary lessons I learned were: You will never be number one in the company for all the right reasons. You have to align your goals and aspirations with that of the company that employs you. You must build others up to build yourself up.

My understanding and execution of those three lessons has served me well throughout the years. I will explain each in more detail in later chapters.

The second mentor

I met Anthony F. during my AYP years. Initially, we met through phone discussions and later in person during meetings. He was the Director of the Mainframe Systems Programming group at the time. I worked within Anthony's department in 1992. I was always amazed at how much he knew. To this day, he is still the best Mainframe guy I have ever come across, in fact, I've yet to come across anyone even remotely close. Anthony was a short, Italian man who was sometimes loud and talked quite a bit with his hands. To say he and I had some very heated moments would be an understatement. Just like Ed Z., I owe Anthony a great deal. He helped me immensely both personally and professionally. He was a perfectionist who cared about doing things right the first time. He focused on the details and the little things that others, including myself, didn't think were a big deal.

Anthony's management style was a bit different from most, but, as my career progressed, I realized his style of management was just what I needed at that time. He was a stickler for documentation, standards, and having clear implementation and back out plans—all our naming standards for a few years were copies of handwritten notes made personally by him. Back then we didn't have Microsoft Word; his penmanship was easy to read, so the notes were simple to follow. If you followed his notes, it was easy to know and quickly find anything.

Anthony's passion and commitment to quality and service was contagious. He is the primary reason customer-focus, service, delivery, and continuous improvement have been four key tenets throughout my career. Those four things personified Anthony. Over time, he not only became my manager and mentor, he became a friend who supported me and gave me good advice during some troubling personal times.

Ed Z. and Anthony F. had a tremendous impact on my professional career. They happened to be individuals who managed me, but your mentor doesn't have to be your boss, they often aren't. I have had other leaders and people I have learned a great deal from.

Outside of family, my friend Darius R. would probably be third behind Ed Z. and Anthony F., in terms of someone I turn to for knowledge, influence, and contributing to my professional and personal growth. He probably doesn't realize he is my mentor—we have been friends for over 20 years. For me it has been a special friendship and I have learned a great deal from him. Whenever I have looked at a new job opportunity or considered making a life-changing decision, the person I was most likely to talk to first was Darius. That is still true today.

Within the last 5 years, Ram C. and Gary N. have been my strongest supporters and mentors. They both pushed and challenged me beyond my comfort zone. I consistently had to learn and adapt while leading teams and taking on new challenges. I grew professionally with every opportunity. Because of the two of them, I am a much stronger manager and leader.

Benefits to having a mentor

First, let me remind you again of what I stated earlier: "*Not everyone can be a knowledge leader, but many qualified leaders can be classified as a mentor.*" A mentor and knowledge leader are not always the same person, although they can be. It takes a special person to be both. My focus here will be solely on mentors.

As a young professional, finding a good mentor should be your first objective. As you grow professionally and personally, you should seek out a strong knowledge leader; someone who can mentor you, but also has the passion and capacity to teach you how to lead. Many strong mentoring relationships provide an opportunity for both parties to learn from each other through developing a caring and respectful partnership. Corporate mentoring programs have long been recognized as an essential strategy for attracting, developing, and retaining top employees. So, if you are an AYP, there is clear evidence you should seek a mentor early in your career. If you come across one equally committed and passionate about teaching you how to lead, then you have found yourself a knowledge leader as well.

Additional mentor benefits:

Insight – A mentor can offer you access to years of experience and knowledge. Mentors can be wonderful for sharing what worked, what didn't, ways to achieve your goals, and help with setting effective objectives. Just when you think you have all the answers, a mentor can point out that you don't! A good mentor's 'been there, done that' influence can be the calm you need in a storm. This is someone you can let your guard down with and ask those stupid questions we all have at one time or another.

Networking – When you have a relationship with a person in the know, you are on your way to successfully networking. A mentor is ideally someone who can introduce you to people outside of your circle, maybe even those you would not normally have access to.

Perspective – A mentor is great for providing perspective. It's all too easy to get caught up in the drama at work! While friends and family may have great advice, a mentor can help keep you grounded and focused on what's important while you create your path to success.

Alliance – Your relationship with your mentor is not like any other. It's a potent combination of teacher, confidant, and cheerleader all rolled into one. The lessons you'll learn will last a lifetime and you will always remember this experience.

How to find a mentor

While some companies are actively involved in creating mentor/mentee relationships (more on that ahead), in many cases you will have to take the lead in seeking a mentor. If you have no idea who to ask, find local organizations active in your community. Find one that resonates with you then take an interest in their leadership. Sometimes all you need is getting together for coffee or having a quick lunch to establish a rapport. You can even join an organization that aligns with your values and take advantage of the networking opportunities.

Another great way to connect with a mentor within your current company is to collaborate on a project. Choose something that supports your potential mentor's efforts and ask for help in putting it together. Having a common goal and collaborating on a project can lead to a deeper relationship during the process.

Building a healthy mentor relationship

While I didn't have formal agreements with either of my mentors, you may choose to establish a more official relationship with yours. To make the most of a mentoring relationship, consider the following:

- Decide how often you will meet—both how frequently and for what length of time. Monthly meetings of an hour or two are common. Some mentoring partners meet or talk often, once a week or daily. While the content and format may vary, each session should highlight what you're trying to achieve and how you are progressing.

- Think of the goals of the relationship—what you would like to learn. Determine the focus and purpose of why you're doing this. Is it to develop a particular skill or create a new career path? Perhaps it is because you are a new employee and want to orient yourself with the company.

- This should never be considered a short cut to the top or an inside track; it is a professional and respectful relationship in which you both can benefit. Never use this as an opportunity to complain or vent about co-workers.

- Sometimes, it's helpful to set an end date so you can part ways easily. There may be a natural end (move to another job or department), but just in case, having an end in sight may allow you to move forward or move on and learn from someone else.

- Remember that mentors are sharing valuable time and insight. Express gratitude for their expertise and leadership skills.

Now it's your turn—how to be a great mentor

In mentorship, it is an unwritten rule that "one should give back at least what they've received." So, if you've ever had a mentor, think about paying it forward. You may have always wished you'd had someone to show you the ropes and now look forward to passing on some of your hard earned wisdom. Helping someone succeed can be incredibly satisfying. I know from my experience how much you gain in return when you mentor someone. There is a great deal of gratification in watching someone you've helped reach full potential. Truthfully, very few things excite me more. Effective mentoring goes both ways: people of different ages with different styles and perspectives can blend their skills and both become better for it. By investing in others around you, you're also investing in yourself and your company. As a mentor, you're on the front lines, able to identify, recruit, and develop new talent. Think of it as contributing to the growth of rising stars!

Ten things you can do to make the most out of your mentoring experience:

1. Be committed. Being a mentor is an obligation so, if you're offering to help someone, follow through on your promise.

2. Always play both roles. Ideally, throughout most of our lives, we are never only a mentor or a mentee. We should all learn from one another and teach each other throughout our careers.

3. Recognize that a mentee can be anyone at any time. It isn't limited to learning from the top down; in today's world, it can also be peer-to-peer relationships across industries. Companies realize that, when people from

different skills and backgrounds come together to collaborate and brainstorm, it can produce amazing results. It's all about the ability to draw knowledge and supplement skill gaps while helping each person learn and grow.

4. Take the time to listen. To provide the best guidance and support, you first must understand the person and the situation. Be able to listen to your mentee vent and work through tough spots. A good mentor spends more time listening than speaking.

5. Ask questions, but don't provide all of the answers. When you're a mentor, it's easy to get caught up in the way things used to be. Remember your goal: to prepare someone to use his or her own brain! You want to ask a lot of open-ended questions so your mentee can learn to fail and succeed on their own.

6. Be compassionate. To provide guidance, you must understand the other person's needs and recognize that you may have a different perspective on situations, given your experience. To give advice that is well received, show concern and empathy.

7. Have patience. Much like parenting, mentoring can be equal parts satisfying and frustrating! It may also take place over a long term. Quick fixes are few and far between, so model patience whenever you can.

8. Be a role model. As a mentor, you are always setting an example. Set the bar as high, or higher, than you'd expect from the person you are mentoring.

9. Lead by example. Your goal is not to simply give advice and guidance, but also to equip your mentee for the future. Words are powerful, but action is impactful. As a mentor, you should live by the adage, "Do as I say AND as I do!"

10. Fully invest yourself in the process. Care about the relationship and resist the temptation to phone in your time and efforts. It takes a genuine interest to develop and nurture another person. Mentees are typically eager, invested, and also vulnerable. When you invest yourself in your mentee, you'll get much more out of the experience. On a side note, if you don't feel it's a good fit from the beginning, it may be better to move on and mentor someone else to avoid getting into a situation where you do more harm than good.

As a mentee seeking an active mentor, one of your core values should be to improve continuously—it's a constant activity that you choose to engage in. When you make personal development a priority, leaders will recognize that and be encouraged to help you grow, you only have to be ready to listen and to learn.

CHAPTER TWO

Align your aspirations for success

As an employee, you must recognize that your individual aspirations and objectives will never rise above those of the company you work for or its customers. You must understand the importance of aligning your aspirations with the objectives of your company, its shareholders, and its customers. In this chapter, we'll explore goal-setting and how to view your career within the context of the much larger picture of the company's ambitions. In this way, you can better prepare and align your skills, set effective goals, outline a clear path for achievement, and quickly recover from temporary setbacks.

The importance of goals

Every business, whether big or small, shares the same projection: success. Setting goals and finding an effective way to align and track those goals can lead to greater success. As an aspiring professional, you too will have your own set of projections: ideas that you'd like to see become reality. The only way you can take a dream and make it reality is to recognize the importance of goal setting. Goals are resolutions designed to achieve the desired result. Short or long-term goals can give a clear understanding of what you are trying to accomplish. Goal-setting is necessary to focus on what is important. Without goals, there is no defined purpose; there is nothing to strive for.

Think of goals as steps on the ladder that lead to success at the top. If you are missing steps, how do you reach the top of the ladder? Missing steps on the ladder will hinder your ability to keep on climbing. When you lack goals, you can become inactive, or find yourself frustrated and unable to achieve results due to the lack of a clear path toward accomplishment. Clear goals and objectives are key to every successful business strategy and must be a critical element of your own professional strategy. Without goals or milestones, how do you measure your growth or success? How do you know if you have achieved each of your objectives? What about setbacks? How will you manage those and continue to march forward? If that step is missing on the ladder, what is your alternative way to reaching the top?

By setting goals, you will have a clear path to your destination and can better endure and overcome setbacks. In fact, setbacks will seem like nothing more than minor detours. Setting goals allows you the safety net of knowing there will always be another way, and knowing you will find it. When your goals are properly selected and realistic, you will reach your destination, even if it's not exactly the way you planned or within the timeframe you had expected.

Setting goals

While working for my first mentor, Ed Z., I found myself in the middle of a frustrating situation. I was offered a position I really wanted but couldn't have. This trainee position (offered by my second mentor, Anthony F.) was exactly what I thought I had been gearing up for all along. I had set a personal goal of achieving this coveted position for years; needless to say, when offered the job, I was more than excited. I felt as though all of my hard work of learning and studying would finally pay off—I had been preparing for my next job for years. I had spent a lot of time and effort developing my skills and preparing myself for such an opportunity. My eye was on the prize! I was ready to go and thought I had done everything within my control to deserve a chance at my dream job. So, you can imagine my disbelief when Ed Z. denied my request to move on.

After my request had been denied, I was filled with an array of negative emotions: shock, anger, betrayal. I felt he and the company were being unfair. I just didn't understand why. I had done everything I thought was necessary to get the promotion and there were three other operators available to do what I did, so it was difficult for me to understand why I could not make the move at that time.

Ed Z. explained that, while my goals were important to me, and my development professionally was important to him as the leader of our department, the goals of the company had priority over my individual aspirations. What he explained was that my exit at that time would create a skill gap for the department because no other operators' skills were equivalent to mine. I had become known for many things in my operator role: stepping forward in a crisis—even with everyone watching; memorizing all procedures, and my ability to shut down or bring up systems quicker than anyone without a manual in front of me. I did my job well, and I was one of the best, if not the best, at it.

No matter how good I was, I couldn't move forward purely for business reasons. My leaving without a properly trained team in place would put the company's objectives of providing the best service to its customers at risk. By not properly training and leading my peers, I hadn't aligned my goals with those of the company. I later realized that it wasn't Ed Z.'s, or the company's, fault I couldn't move on, it was mine. By not training the others, I held myself back. When I set my goals, I should have aligned them with company objectives from the start. If I had, I would have ensured that other operators learned what I had learned and could provide the same level of service. As the lead operator, I should have put in place a succession plan that would provide some level of continuity. You may be thinking, *wouldn't that have been the job of your supervisor?* Good question. The short answer is my supervisor at the time wasn't looking to move anywhere, I was. I had to own my plan and do what was necessary to reach my destination—my dream job. I didn't, and I lost out on an opportunity to take a role I had wanted for years.

Types of goals

Goals can be short-term or long-term. Effective goal setting should always include a good mix of both short and long-term initiatives. There is basically no downside to setting goals. Think of short-term goals as pit stops along the way on a long journey. Pit stops allow you to assess how far you have come and how much further you have to go to reach your destination. It is a way of evaluating your achievements and failures without ever losing sight of the big picture. When you set long-term goals, you are setting your final destination. Once that is done, you have only to navigate through the setbacks and failures to arrive. Just know that no path will be straight nor will it be smooth. Expect a long and rough ride. But I promise you, it will be worth it.

Four reasons you should make setting goals a priority:

Measurement. Always strive to improve, grow, and make impactful personal and professional gains. The clearest way to measure success is to set goals and work towards them. Establishing goals allows you to measure where you've been and where you are while keeping the big picture in perspective.

Unity. Good goal setting occurs when your objectives enable you to achieve your goals—you know when you will cross the finish line. This helps eliminate confusion and uncertainty. When your goals and objectives are clearly understood, it creates a foundation for decision-making. Once Ed Z. explained the reason behind why he wasn't allowing me to move on, I was able to step back and see my part in the overall plan. I then went back and readjusted my goals and objectives to align with those of the company.

Definition. Information is power; the more you know, the better your decisions will be. With well-defined goals, there is a better understanding and ability to maintain focus. If developing a stronger team of operators would enable me to pursue my goals and help the company at the same time, I was all for it.

Reassessment. When you set goals early and make a habit of continually monitoring them, you can modify your objectives as necessary. I was able to reassess my own goals in light of my new objectives: train the operators in some of the skill sets that only I possessed and then I could move on to my next goal.

What do great goals look like?

When creating a goal, S-M-A-R-T is an effective and well-documented framework that is very easy to remember. Any goal (s) you set should follow the S-M-A-R-T principles. They should be:

Specific: Well defined and easy to manage objectives

Measurable: Track and measure your progress

Attainable: Set the bar high, but not too high—make sure your goals are realistic

Relevant: Focus on goals that will give you the biggest impact

Timely: Establish a guideline—goals without deadlines can be overlooked

Another aspect of setting goals is being clear on your objectives and your road to success. They have to be YOURS: *You Own Understanding the Reality of Success.* Said differently, using YOURS also could mean:

- Goals are something *you* define

- Outcomes are something that you will *own*

- Only you know and *understand* your motivation

- Only you must live with the *reality* of success or failure

- You must be determined and committed to *succeed*

Great goal setting is when you keep the amount of goals manageable. Having an unmanageable set of goals can have a negative effect, causing you to spin your wheels or derail your progress toward achieving any of them.

When I knew I needed to shift my focus and change my goals, I resisted at first. It was difficult for me to see the big picture, all I saw was my vision going up in smoke. I didn't stop to think about how moving on would affect the company's overall objectives. I didn't understand all that, I just thought I was being held back from achieving my goals.

After I settled down and had time to think, I learned my next lesson under Ed. Z., I had to build others up in order to build myself up. Great goal setting is done both for business results and personal development. As Ed Z. taught me, goals provide a framework for accountability, and we all need to be equally invested in achieving the desired results. It was time for me to align my goals with those of the company so we could both achieve what we desired.

Aligning goals with company strategies

Goal alignment is critical to your personal and business success. It ensures that you can see the direction of the business and know how your role fits in with the grand scheme of things. When you understand your individual goals and how they relate to the larger goals of your company, you become more engaged at work.

With everyone working together toward the same objectives, it makes leadership stronger and creates organizational flexibility. I needed to get on board with training the operators around me so I could, in turn, move on with my personal goals. I also needed to remember the overall goals of the company. For my area, that always meant having well trained operators who could handle their functions effectively while providing the best service possible.

I was being held accountable as the senior operator. All the time I was learning and growing, making plans for my next goal, and perfecting my skills, I had lost sight of my ultimate responsibilities. I had failed to lead and bring the others with me. Not only had I potentially jeopardized the company's overall effectiveness, I had also shortchanged the other operators. I was not leading them or helping them develop their skills. In not doing so, I put my own personal plans at risk and missed an opportunity for the promotion I dreamed about.

I learned a very valuable lesson. I realized it's important for me to create personal goals that align and support company goals and objectives. I recognized the value in linking with others because the success of my goals depends on the success of my co-workers. For my own individual success and the success of the company, I had to ensure there was an operator (or operators) who could be relied on for their knowledge and expertise, just as they had relied on me for mine.

Motivation when a goal gets off track

During the time I was living with the reality that I would not be able to move on to my dream job, I felt disappointed and unmotivated. I felt I had been unfairly passed over for the promotion. It had taken some time before I could see my career within the context of a much larger picture at work. Nevertheless, I knew I had to get back on track. I began to focus on what mattered and what could help me get to where I wanted to be. Being in the state I was in, I realized that I was not helping myself. I had no choice but to get back into the game, adjust my strategy, and compete again with a purpose.

You will most likely experience the same feeling at least once in your career. When you are unmotivated, work becomes just that: work! You never want that to be the case. Remember, you don't want to just work, you aspire to have a career. To do so, you have to remain motivated as much as possible, all the time.

Here are some ways to shift focus and get back on track:

Stop caring about the wrong things

Yes, I know this is a bold statement, so let me explain. Obviously you need to care about the people you work with and the work you do. What you don't need to focus on are decisions made at the top that don't resonate with you. Once I realized that Ed Z.'s decision meant I couldn't have the job I had been working for, I couldn't let bitterness hinder my job performance. I needed to care about the operators and figure out how I could help them. I didn't need to care about how disappointed I was. Caring about the wrong thing does not serve you in the long run. It accomplishes nothing and can drain your motivation. Instead, I focused on what was within my control.

Work smart

I still had work to do and a future to reconsider—these are not necessarily the same thing! To stay motivated in the present, I focused on the task at hand. I needed to do my job well, which involved building a network of operators who knew my knowledge and expertise and would know how to work effectively. I put my blinders on and focused on building others up so I could be built up in return.

Attitude is everything

I understood I needed to do the work that mattered most to the company and its customers, as well as the team. I had to focus on the work and identify it from the rest of the noise. Once I did that, I was able to gain better focus and stay motivated for longer periods of time. I could then transfer that enthusiasm on to other operators, so they could see the importance of attitude. As disappointed as I was, my attitude remained professional. I was not only proud of the work the operators could perform on behalf of the company, I was proud of who I had become—I discovered my passion for developing others. I remained true to my new objective: to build others up while aligning my aspirations with those of the company.

CHAPTER THREE

Build up others so you can build up yourself

In your careers, it's easy to get so focused on the destination you are trying to reach that you lose sight of the path in front of you. Sometimes your ability to train and develop others will determine how fast you travel the path and reach your destination. Helping others grow is a sure sign of leadership, but doing so may also help you create opportunities for yourself. In this chapter, we discuss the benefits of building others up to create opportunities for yourself.

Share your knowledge

When I was passed over for a promotion, I had to readjust my focus so I could maintain my motivation. In all the time I had spent learning all there was to know about my job and all I could learn about the job I wanted, I failed to train and build my co-workers up. As I stated previously, I cheated myself out of an opportunity by not doing so. I had been so focused on my goals that the team as a whole was set up for failure. Once I recognized what I had done to myself and the department, a light bulb went off! I needed to get those guys caught up quickly so I wouldn't miss my next opportunity. I went back and trained the team vigorously, with intent and purpose—built them up in order to build myself up and move on to my dream job.

You have to reach out and build up as you move forward; otherwise you risk leaving the company in worse shape than when you found it. The goal is to build a deep bench where all of the players, with their different skill sets and strengths, can be relied on to carry out the objectives of the business. I became my co-workers' mentor and coach. They began to look to me for guidance, support, and knowledge. While I was mentoring them, I was also growing as a person and leader. I benefitted immensely from mentoring my team and so will you!

Reasons you should always mentor others:

- You must give in order to receive. Networks of people working together can be highly complex, especially in a team situation similar to the one I was in. Trust the process, and while the effect may take time to build and grow, the results (such as having a well-trained team) are lasting.

- You've heard the expression, "What goes around comes around." Think of building someone up as karma in business. Strengthening a department or area tends to produce positive outcomes (either individually or as a group). Helpfulness is often repaid in reputation and trust. Once I invested my time and talent to get my guys up to speed, I was rewarded with another opportunity for promotion. I already had a good connection with my mentor Ed Z., and now my good reputation had been further established by cause and effect. By giving my time and talents to build my team, I found that people gravitated toward me. Helping others extended beyond my own personal victories, allowing me to establish connections with high-quality contacts within the company.

- Companies suffer when individuals have trouble accessing knowledge they need to do the job effectively. Knowledge hoarding can cripple an organization because it causes weakness and distrust among employees. By not building up others in my area, I was, in effect, diluting the effectiveness of my team, which could have had a disastrous effect on the company as a whole.

Recognize where you are with your peers—if you need to lead, do so

I've also learned that a successful organization needs all kinds of people. The doers can take a vision and make it happen, the managers are skilled in bringing out the best in people and keeping things on track, and the leaders can set the framework in place and motivate others to action. When I stepped up and began building up my team, I started the process of leadership development. I went from a doer who became a manager and, hopefully, emerged as an inspirational leader.

Leadership qualities can be developed no matter where you are within your company. You need no specific title or position (more on this in Chapter 12) to bring vision and encouragement to your co-workers.

Five tips for developing your potential leadership skills:

- Be great at your current job. Make sure you're excelling at whatever you're doing now.

- Observe and listen. Pay attention to the people around you and above you in the organization. Notice what works and what doesn't.

- Step up. If you have a vision, do what you can to share it. If you see a way to improve something, do what you can to make it happen.

- Be willing to evolve. Be humble enough to acknowledge your weaknesses and open to working toward strengthening those areas in which you fall short.

- Be patient with yourself and others. It's been a process for me to transition from a hands-on doer to a manager and a leader. I've made plenty of mistakes, so it's important I give the people who work for me room to try things and not be afraid to fail. As I said in a previous chapter, everyone will fail or face setbacks trying to reach their destination. The key is to learn from every one of your failures.

Good leaders share power

Be committed to helping others when you build someone up. Good leaders develop a powerful team by sharing power, not by focusing on keeping all of the power for themselves.

The leaders who inspire me most are those who make people feel valued. They realize we are all diverse talents, and we each have different roles and varying ways to contribute. When we work together and share the challenges that arise, it's a win-win situation. You end up with an army of people equipped to work independently but also achieve great results as a team.

Being the best doesn't mean anything if you can't share how you became the best with others. Here are some practical ways I have seen the difference play out:

1. Spend personal time with your co-workers in the trenches. This helps you understand and value all aspects of your respective teams. It also lets you see what areas people must develop to strengthen the team.

2. Communicate often. Make it a point to share as much information as possible. A well-informed team can contribute more because they know more.

3. Building a strong team is a much more reliable approach to achieving success—and it gives you more real power in the end. Not only was my department stronger and more capable by the time I finished

training them, I was also rewarded with an opportunity to excel in a different position. I brought my experience with building others up, in order to build myself up, to every new role I have taken since that time.

4. Challenge your peers to challenge themselves to do better and be better.

5. Be creative and constructive in how you regard others and how you help them. Being defensive and making assumptions limits options and growth. Effective leaders win people over by building an open environment of trust and respect. They create meaning for people so they can feel proud of their work. They offer personal recognition. They go out of their way to make the work matter to those doing it.

I was very fortunate to have two Knowledge Leaders who showed me you could succeed in business by sharing your knowledge and respecting the process. There are so many examples of leaders who go the other way and focus on their own climb up the corporate ladder instead of developing those around them. Without good role models, I may have believed that was necessary. I now know the truth and so do you!

Make sure you have a succession plan

When employees in critical roles leave a company, they take with them key knowledge and critical skills. Having a strong succession plan in place is key to a company's longevity.

When a person is promoted and leaves behind a weak or ineffective team, the company will suffer from a lack of skilled workers to fill in any gaps. As was the case in my situation, the number one reason I was held back from a promotion was because of the need for a succession plan.

A succession plan identifies those key positions that will require leadership and the ability to develop and build up others. I had worked hard to know all I could about the job I was doing, but I had not spent enough time reaching out to those around me to make sure they were well trained, too. By identifying me as a leader and holding me accountable to those leadership duties, the company was ensuring continuity. Succession planning is critical to the short-term and long-term success of any organization.

There is no 'one size fits all' succession planning process. Succession plans must be developed according to an organization's business needs and priorities. My Knowledge Leader, Ed Z., knew it was critical that my team be trained and developed before I could vacate my Lead Operator position. He took the necessary steps to implement a succession plan.

It doesn't matter what type of industry or what stage of development your organization is in, succession planning is essential. Whenever you are in a position to build others up, here are a few steps you can take to ensure you have a sustainable succession plan in place:

- Acknowledge the importance of having a plan. What matters is that there is a plan in place specifying who will fill a vacant position, as well as how to identify and develop high-quality leadership and encourage employee commitment.

- Make sure everyone is in sync. The succession plan must be linked to and supported by the overall mission and vision of the company.

- Act with a sense of determination and commitment. Ed Z.'s focus was on building a deep bench. He was committed to creating a well-trained department.

- Take action and be honest about the need for personnel who will build others up. The focus should be on developing a strong team for your organization that will help others grow.

- The common thread for executing a successful succession plan is communication. Ed Z. let me know why I wasn't moving forward and what I needed to do to make that happen.

- Understand that succession planning is difficult and it does not happen overnight. It takes commitment, persistence, collaboration, and lots of hard work to ensure its success.

CHAPTER FOUR

Recognize your IDEAL situation

You encounter all types of personalities in the workplace. As you move along the fast track of your career, you're bound to work with a wide variety of them. And while it may be tempting to try to make everyone fit into a basic personality mold, effective leadership respects that each employee is different. Deal with different personalities head on as a leader to strengthen and contribute to your team. In order to be successful, you must also recognize who will support your personal and professional objectives and who will be inhibitors to achieving them.

A few years ago, I began to take note of the different personalities and traits I had come across while working with and leading various groups. As I discussed these traits with others, I noticed there were certain 'types' that surfaced most often.

This chapter covers the importance of recognizing the people around you and establishing who is for you or against you, who the team players are, and who the achievers and leaders are. Recognizing and differentiating between these basic personality traits will enable you to understand who to align with and who to stay away from within the workforce. Remember, you are who you choose to follow.

As an AYP, you will benefit greatly from understanding the dynamics behind what makes up your current team and other individuals who may be contributors or inhibitors to your ideal situation.

"The strength of the team is each individual member. The strength of each member is the team" —**Phil Jackson**

Different types of personalities

To better understand the people around you, I've created five dimensions of the personalities I typically come across. In my experience, if you take time to notice the diversity and varying characteristics of those who fall within the five dimensions outlined below, you will learn how they differ and how some can hurt you while others will be enablers of your success.

Influencers – These are the people who can help you or cause havoc for you. Depending on your age, you may or may not recall the vintage EF Hutton commercial that used to run in the 80s. Anyone who was around during that time should remember that, "When E.F. Hutton talks, people listen." Influencers are like EF Hutton—when they have something to share, others will listen. The key is to know whether what they are saying supports you or negatively impacts you. If what they say supports you, you'll want to align with them quickly, especially if others in high places think highly of them. That is usually a good indication they can teach or help you in many ways.

If the influencer is against you or is just one of those people who always is negative about something, you will recognize them; they are never satisfied and nothing ever seems to be good enough—co-workers, the company and its leaders, products, you name it. They are simply never happy with anything. Spreading rumors also seems to be a sport to them. Unfortunately, these types of influencers have followers too. Misery loves company, so they will always recruit others of the same mindset. Run as far away from this type of influencer as quickly as possible. This type of influencer will ultimately become a distractor to your team and to your company. They rarely adapt to changing company dynamics and therefore aren't around long enough to see how things work out either.

Distractors – This personality type is an inhibitor to anything you are trying to achieve. For them, nothing will ever be right, and *you* will never be right, no matter what you do. These people are a distraction—either with their conduct or their attitude. They can be a destructive force and will hurt your progress if you waste time accommodating their negative behavior. Avoid distractors at all costs. They usually go beyond just having a pet peeve with a co-worker—they are often merely difficult people to deal with *all of the time*. Learn early on who these people are and clue in to the responses of those around them. Difficult people can be managed; difficult people with their own agenda can't be changed. To have success, distractors need to be spotted early on and avoided, or they will hurt you and the productivity of your entire team.

Enablers – These personalities are also called worker bees. They are the backbone of every operation, and everyone needs them. When you need help, they will typically respond, "Tell me what you need me to do!" They are great co-workers and team players. These are the people you need to get to know because you will need their help, most likely before they will need yours. You will also learn many good traits from them. Most enablers I have met are humble and have little aspirations to do more than what they are currently doing; not because they aren't driven— they are. They are just satisfied and happy with what they do. If you are looking to move up, enablers are perfect resources for you. Enablers will rarely be your competition, so they will be more willing to share. The key is to build a relationship with them and appreciate their contributions. In my experience, I have found that enablers like to be appreciated and praised more often than being publicly recognized.

Achievers – These are the 'go to' people when something really must get done and done right. They are driven by results—they will let nothing get in the way of achieving their objective. If you want a progressive career, watch and learn from this group of people. When you want to be the best, learn from the best. Achievers are highly motivated and take their work seriously. People in this category will be your competition—most are like you, they have their eyes set on bigger things. Find them and learn from them. Generally, the people in this category become leaders within the company in some capacity.

Leaders – These people may or may not be in a formal leadership role, but are looked upon as leaders by their co-workers and others within an organization. As an AYP, your goal is to be amongst this group. Other workers look up to them and management respects their views and usually makes plans to groom them for other progressive roles. Since everyone already looks up to them and turns to them for guidance, giving them more responsibility would be an expected occurrence.

The best people within this dimension will have established reputations beyond their current department. Many people will know them and senior managers and leaders from across the company usually know of their work and accomplishments.

You will find that most people in this group have many things in common, one being that almost all of them will have been mentored by someone. So, if you must, go back to Chapter One for a refresher of why having a mentor is so important.

"You have to get along with people, but you also have to recognize that the strength of a team is different people with different perspectives and different personalities." —**Steve Case**

How to Work with Different Personality Traits

To become better at understanding the people around you, watch the behavior of the five dimensions and get to know how they differ. Use that understanding to predict how these individuals will react to various situations. You can also use this knowledge to observe tasks, projects, or settings to better understand which situations will cause people to excel or fail.

Combining multiple personalities on a team, or in a department, can improve productivity and lead to new ideas, however, without proper consideration, the same combination can result in communication breakdown, conflict, and less productivity. I've found there are a few ways to bring different types of people to work together—for you, the trick is to view each person individually and maintain a positive relationship.

There is often more than one way to approach and complete work within a team. Different personality types perform better in different situations. For example, the achiever may be able to run with a project with little supervision while the enabler needs some guidance. Again, you need to figure out where and how you fit within such a team or lead such a diverse team.

One thing you can control is how well you perform your tasks. If you find your distractors taking away from your productivity, kindly let them know and refocus on the task at hand. Every team should have diversity, but not everyone will be a team player. Gravitate towards the team players and distance yourself from the distractors.

Evaluating how you view people who disagree with you is also important. Do you try to understand the basis for their views? Do you work toward mutual understanding? Do you illicit the opinion of others? Having a disagreement with co-workers and team members is not a bad thing. Sometimes, you will not all be on the same page. That's okay and it will happen. The key is for you not to take it personally and remained focused on the objective. Doing so will help you establish a great rapport with members within your organization. No one wants to work with someone who doesn't know how to agree to disagree and sort out a mutual conclusion.

"Individual commitment to a group effort—that is what makes a team work, a company work, a society work, a civilization work." — **Vince Lombardi**

Know who the players are and build from there

Continually grow and keep moving on—the key is to continue to gain knowledge and propel yourself forward. Find out who the key players are and grow with their help.

Get to know your co-workers and managers. Take an interest in their lives, experiences, special occasions, and so on. Be willing to share similar information about yourself. Again, it is all about building relationships and trust. People trust others who are willing to share.

CHAPTER FIVE

Don't just talk to your neighbor, talk to everyone

These days, it isn't just about who you know, but who knows you—at work, among other professionals (both within and outside of your industry), and within your community. Building relationships is the key to your success.

In this chapter, we will explore the importance of networking and how effective networking can help you develop professionally and be an enabler to a successful career. You should network with the purpose of building a team of contacts and mentors. If those you network with aren't helping you propel your career forward in some way, you haven't networked well.

Networking

Networking is the act of meeting with like-minded individuals for a common cause or purpose. Networking can occur anywhere and you may not share a common interest with other person. Networking is ultimately about building a pipeline of contacts and relationships that may be of benefit to either party or both. Networking is an art. Some are masters at it and others dread the notion of meeting new people altogether.

Have you ever stood in a room at a large networking event and just people watched? If you took a moment to look around the room, you would notice there are always two kinds of interactions occurring. Some people seem to know almost everyone—they 'work the room', shaking hands and moving from group to group easily. They greet everyone with a smile and leave no hand unshaken. Others, meanwhile, either stand by themselves or stand clustered in small groups, refusing to mingle. They look uncomfortable, counting the minutes until they can go home. Which type of interaction do you think gets more done? Which of the two types is building a contact pipeline? Now ask yourself why. The reason is simple: your ability to relate well to others, no matter the situation, will determine how effectively you can network.

Why networking is important

As I said earlier, networking is about who you know and who knows you. The more people you know and are known to, the better your pipeline of contacts and acquaintances, contacts that can someday be beneficial to both you and them. The fact is none of us knows everyone. If you can't know everyone, then know enough people who can help broaden your reach beyond your immediate friends and associates.

The three key benefits to networking for professional reasons are:

- Access to mentors

- Job opportunities

- Professional development

Networking with a variety of individuals—colleagues, customers, professional peers, community-based organizations, and even competitors—will play a part in your success. Sometimes your professional advancement may depend on your ability to network with a diverse group of people. The people whose help you need may even be found in a different part of your organization or at another company.

Smart networking helps your career

If you connect with colleagues in different areas of your organization, they may keep you in the loop when job opportunities arise. By networking, you may find your next mentor, friend, or spouse—you never know. That actually occurs often these days. Smart networking means building strong and mutually beneficial relationships that last. Smart networking is also about networking long before you have a need. Too often I have seen people attend networking meetings after they have lost a job. In my opinion, that is too late. You should network regardless of your employment status. Waiting until you are unemployed to do so doesn't help you.

When networking, most tend to associate with others like them. This is not the smart thing to do. To build a strong and deep bench of mentors for your career team, step outside your comfort zone and seek a wide and diverse spectrum of individuals whose background, culture, experience, and attitude may differ from yours, but whose character and leadership traits you admire.

Networking in today's world is often digital, so face-to-face isn't the only way to network anymore. At all times, you are close to important information, resources and people either physically or online. Think about it, many studies have demonstrated that we all know an average of a few thousand people directly, and each of those people has a similar number of contacts. Don't believe me? Look at your LinkedIn profile, if you have one; look at your direct connects and then their connections. Do you get the picture? Just a few well-placed phone calls or emails to friends—and friends of friends—can get you in touch with almost anybody in the world. Odds are if you don't know someone, someone in your network of friends or their friends will. Clearly, the resources and mechanisms to build a supportive network of acquaintances, mentors, and general contacts is always within reach, the question is how do you network effectively?

Effective Networking

Relationships are a basic human need. Helping other people fulfill their need for relationships helps you, too. Here are some tips on forming lasting connections, both at work and in your personal life.

1. Talk. If you want to make friends at work, you have to talk to other people. If you want people to like you, or at least get to know you, you must be willing to open up and have conversations.

2. Listen. In this busy world, a good listener can be hard to find. If you are able to listen and to empathize with what other people are saying, you'll very likely draw people to you.

3. Join Groups. Seek out professional groups to join or look for opportunities to expand your involvement in social groups. Check out what's available and find the group that best suits your needs and interests.

4. Move out of your comfort zone. Many times, people start a new job and meet two or three people whom they work with directly. Rather than branching out to other departments, they stick with the group they already know. If you want to make friends at work, you need to break out of your comfort zone and do things that will allow you to get to know others who work within your organization. Again, it isn't who you know, but who knows you.

5. 'Do' Lunch. Breaks are a great way to get to know your fellow workers, particularly on lunch breaks, if you happen to work nine to five. Lunch is where people talk and share their personal lives and, every now and then, their professional aspirations.

6. Volunteer. Volunteering can be a valuable tool in helping you meet and make friends. Whether it's volunteering for projects outside of your area or for things that happen outside of work but involve co-workers, make volunteering a habit.

7. Include Others. Another way to make friends at work is to include others in what you are doing. If you want help, ask for it. Be sure to introduce yourself to new employees, they will be looking to meet new people.

Effective networking depends on managing your personal and professional relationships in three directions: up with your boss or mentors; down with those coming up behind you; and laterally, with your peers. In all three directions, effective networking means that you identify key relationships, build mutual understanding and act in ways that benefit both sides.

Network for career opportunities

Networking is a two-way street that involves making connections and sharing information. It is a way of relating to others, not a technique for calling in favors or landing a job. However, there are some ways you can maximize your networking in regards to looking for a new job.

Be real. In any job search or networking situation, being you—the real you—should always be your goal. Pursuing what you want, and not what you think others will like, will be more fulfilling and ultimately more successful.

Be respectful. If you're reconnecting with an old friend or colleague, take time to get through the catching-up phase before you cut to the chase. If this person is a busy professional you don't know well, be considerate of his or her time and come straight out with your request.

Seek advice. You want your contacts to become allies in your job search, not make them feel ambushed. So instead of asking for a job directly, ask for information or guidance. They may refer you or have just the opportunity you are looking for.

Be specific. Before you get fired up and try to reconnect with everyone you've ever known, get your act together. Do your homework and prepare what you will say. Are you looking for a reference or seeking an introduction? Always make sure your resume and qualifications are up to date so you can provide current professional experience.

Don't rush! Effective networking is best done when focused, not hurried. Just because you have an agenda does not mean you need to rush when making a connection. To successfully network, remind yourself to slow down and enjoy the process. The laid back approach is more conducive to building a relationship of mutual support.

Be thankful. Don't be someone who connects, gets what they want, and disappears until the next time you need something. Invest in your network by following up and providing feedback to those who were kind enough to offer their help. Thank them and inform them if you got the job or interview. If you don't have success or need more help, it's easier to reach out when you've been open and kept the communication flowing.

Share the wealth. The next time you see an opportunity that seems like a great fit for someone else, share that information. Be generous with your time and contacts when it comes to helping others.

Networking is just the beginning

Going to an event or giving out a few business cards isn't enough. To really be effective, go beyond networking. Think of it this way: networking may provide a connection, but follow-ups build the bridge. A bridge gets you from point A to point B. A contact you don't follow up with may never become a part of your network.

Steps to ensure you are making the most of your networking efforts and building bridges

Check old emails: Go through old contacts you may have forgotten you had. Check for press releases or mail you may have filed away to look for a connection to a business or individual you are interested in. Take the time to clean out and organize your inbox periodically in search of potential contacts.

Always have business cards: You never know when you will run into someone, so always have business cards on hand. Get in the habit of passing out two cards to anyone you meet:

one for them and one for someone they think may potentially contact you for business.

Take notes: When someone gives you their card, take a moment to write down a quick note about the person. In your follow-up, you can mention the specifics of your conversation. Don't just rely on your memory. Keep a log of all your interactions—who, what, where, and why.

Take risks, reach out: don't limit your contacts to people you meet in person. You may meet someone online through a blog or admire someone's article. The worst thing that can happen is they don't answer or they say no. The sky is the limit on the best thing that could happen!

Identify needs: Find any areas where you need to build your contacts and seek connections in those areas. Work to improve your critical relationships. Think of what other people need and find ways you can help them do their jobs better. Fill the gaps.

Remember that networking is a lifelong project! Get used to continuously reviewing and evaluating your connections and how you network.

CHAPTER SIX

Satisfy the customer to progress

"The purpose of a business is to create a customer." — **Peter Drucker**

Let's face it, no matter what your occupation, the best measurement of how well you are doing will always be tied to how well you've satisfied your customers. There is always a direct link between business success and customer satisfaction. Whenever I speak about this topic, I always start out by mentioning the obvious: show me one business without a customer. It's not possible, as there's not one business that exists without one! This goes for you as well. You have customers and you cannot succeed if your customers are dissatisfied. In your case, your customers won't go to another business, they will just work with another person. That isn't a good thing either.

Customer perception will always be your reality. It sometimes hurts, but businesses and individuals like yourself will always need the customer; the customer won't always need you or the business.

This chapter covers the relevance of being customer-focused and how that focus contributes to a progressive and rewarding career.

It is not the employer who pays the wages. Employers only handle the money. It is the customer who pays the wages. —**Henry Ford**

Who is a customer?

You may consider your customer to be the person who pays your company for the products and services it provides. But also, as a provider within your company, you have customers too. If you are in information technology, finance, real estate, the mailroom, or almost any other profession, you have customers. Your customers could be your co-workers, managers, executives, or someone from various areas or groups you support or provide a service to.

If you provide a service to someone, regardless of the service, that person is your customer. Whether it is getting the payroll printed so the mailroom can distribute them on time or setting up a computer on a co-worker's desk so they can be productive, those are services you are providing to your customer. Just because they don't write your company a check for goods or services provided, that doesn't mean you should view them as any less than your paying customers. They, too, can have a positive or adverse impact on how you are paid or even how long you are employed.

When you are in corporate America, you have to believe that everything you do for your co-worker, manager, or senior executive is ultimately for the benefit of the paying customer—the ones who enable your company to write you a check and provide for your family. In every business, whomever pays, rules! Your number one goal in business is to satisfy these customers. To do so, you not only have to satisfy that group directly but indirectly as well by helping others that may work with them directly—your internal customers. Your paying customers are satisfied when you and others within your organization do your part to meet their expectations consistently—it will always take a team.

Some simple yet important things you should keep in mind to remember in relation to customers:

- Customers enable you to collect a salary—weekly, bi-weekly, or monthly

- Without customers there is no revenue or means for your company to pay expenses (your pay is one of those expenses), no revenue means no employment

- When customers are satisfied they buy more of your products and services, in turn, your investors will invest more, which means opportunities for higher wages and more jobs

- When you satisfy your customers, you set yourself up for recognition and additional opportunities to do more and take on roles with more responsibility, which can benefit you financially

Benefits of customer satisfaction

Let's talk about how we would describe a typical paying customer of a company who purchases goods and services, and the effects they have on a company's reputation as well as its revenue and profit outcomes.

A satisfied customer is one who becomes your supporter—they return for repeat business. A very satisfied customer will tell others, creating referrals for you and your company. That means an organization will have a source of continuous referrals and new business. Word-of-mouth marketing is the most cost-effective form of marketing you will ever have.

Now, let's put this same experience in the context of how it applies to you in your professional career. As I stated, a satisfied customer becomes your supporter—for you, there is nothing better than a co-worker, manager, or senior executive singing your praises. The more they tell others about your performance and work, the more recognition you will get throughout the company. As the praise broadens, your network of supporters expands and more people learn who you are. I stated earlier that the greatest form of marketing for any business is word-of-mouth. The same applies to you. The more people who talk about their positive customer experience with you, the more opportunities you will have. So, by simply satisfying the customer(s), you satisfy yourself.

After all the praise, the verbal recognition comes next. Finally, there may be a form of financial recognition or a promotion for the work you have performed.

On the other side of the spectrum are paying customers who aren't satisfied with the quality of the products, the service, or both. The biggest problem here is that only a small percentage of the dissatisfied customers will file a complaint with the company. If services continue to be below expectations, they will discontinue using your products and services and find another provider. It's well-known that most dissatisfied customers will not tell you they had a bad experience, he/she will instead share their dissatisfaction with a multitude of others. With the reach of the Internet in play, that number rapidly increases and now news spreads to hundreds of thousands with just one click of a button. Today, a tweet can go viral in seconds and just like that you and your company could be hit with an avalanche of negative publicity.

In the context of your professional career, when your internal customers are dissatisfied, they too will complain. Unlike the paying dissatisfied customers, your internal customers will make sure you know they are dissatisfied—believe me, they will make sure you know about it. You will be made aware through direct feedback, phone calls, and escalations to your supervisor, and in writing—mostly via email. Last, but most importantly, they will share their dissatisfaction with others within the organization. When that repeatedly occurs, everyone will know you, but for all the wrong reasons.

Spend a lot of time talking to customers face to face. You'd be amazed how many companies don't listen to their customers.—**Ross Perot**

Overlooking the importance of strong customer relationships and not ensuring positive customer experiences will be detrimental to your career. I cannot emphasize this enough. You won't be perfect, none of us are, but perfection should be the intent. I always say, as a provider of services, that I am committed to "delivering on the promise of service."

To me, when you agree to provide a service, you are making a promise to provide that service based on customer expectations whether or not a contract exists between you and the customer. I have failed many times on delivering on my promise, so will you. Nonetheless, I always made every effort to immediately correct anything I fell short on, and so should you. Customers like it when you take accountability and not only admit that you fell short of your promise, but also convey a plan to address the issue and make certain the same thing doesn't occur again. Make sure you don't find yourself constantly apologizing; that would be a sure indication you rarely live up to delivering on your promise of service.

All customers, regardless of what class (paying, co-worker, manager, etc.), are demanding and their expectations of you as a service provider will continue to increase. If you do things well today, they will expect you to do them better tomorrow; if you are very responsive today, the expectation tomorrow is that you will be faster. If your service comes with a cost today, tomorrow they will want that same service at a much lower cost. So, the theme of better, faster, and cheaper with the same level of quality and service is something you should imprint into your mind—you will hear it many times in several different ways throughout your career.

A few basic rules of customer service

Honesty is the Best Policy – As I mentioned earlier, accountability is important. Always be honest and own up to mistakes and missteps. Communicate with customers about how you will fix the mistake and work to ensure you don't make the same mistake twice.

Response Time – Respond to customer inquiries and concerns. If an error is made, the best way to handle it is to immediately get on the phone to the customer to explain the mistake. Even better, if you are in physical proximity to the customer, pay them a personal visit. They will appreciate that. Offer frequent updates if there is a prolonged issue with the service you are providing and periodically give them a brief update on progress to give them some level of confidence that you are aware of the impact on them, then reassure them it has your full attention.

Be Realistic – Customers who have been promised something that isn't delivered are apt to be frustrated and disappointed. In other words, under-promise and over-deliver whenever possible! This may take some wrangling with some customers who want things fast, but when doing it right crosses with just getting it done on time, always do it right. The customer may be upset initially, but they will thank you for it later.

No Customers = No Company – You should love your customers. Always respect and appreciate your customers no matter what. Sometimes it will be difficult because many are demanding—remember that, ultimately, they pay your bills or help you further your career. Never forget, everyone you provide a service to, either within your department, outside of your department, or external individuals who pay for products and services your company provides, is your customer.

How to build customer satisfaction

How do you ensure your customers are getting the attention they deserve? How do you satisfy the customer in order to satisfy yourself?

A few basic principles you can focus on to build a higher level of overall satisfaction: both for the customers and for you

Be customer service oriented: Stop by someone's office or pick up the phone and make a call, just to check in. Return calls and emails on a timely basis. If there is a problem, always describe the problem and offer a plan to address the issue and, whenever possible, offer a timeframe in which you plan to correct the problem.

Focus on the customer experience: Remember why you have a job and why your company is in business—you both exist to serve and satisfy your customers.

Develop a clear understanding of the customer's expectations: How can you best meet their requirements? What do they expect in terms of service, delivery and continuous improvement? Always be focusing on how to get better, faster, and provide your services at a lower cost if applicable.

Develop relationships: Just like in a personal relationship, your relationship with your customers must be nurtured and developed. This can include such things as: having regular meetings to ensure expectations are being met, offering planning or customer-focused meetings to understand changing customer needs, having casual conversations to get to know your co-workers beyond work. Such things help to build rapport and, potentially, friendship. A large group of my friends have been co-workers and customers of mine in the past.

There is only one boss. The customer. And he can fire everybody in the company from the chairman on down, simply by spending his money somewhere else.—**Sam Walton**

The reason I titled this chapter, "Satisfy the customer to progress" is because satisfying the customer is the best way for you to satisfy yourself. Doing business with people is more than just doing business. Customers drive a business and your career.

Sam Walton, the founder of Walmart, once said, "There is only one boss: the customer." No one could have said it any better.

CHAPTER SEVEN

If you aren't being challenged, you aren't growing.

As an AYP, you should be looking to grow, to not only want more but also do more. During your AYP years, your objective is to develop new skills and determine your future career path. To develop, you constantly have to move beyond your comfort zone. Take on assignments and projects that are new to you. Exposure to new and diverse work assignments provides a broad range of direct experience. It also provides you with challenges you will need to grow. New things will constantly test your ability to adapt and learn. You cannot grow if you remain comfortable in a current role. You should never get comfortable; always get challenged.

Challenge yourself every day to do better and be better. Growth starts with a decision to move beyond your present circumstances. — **Robert Tew**

Work plays a significant role in our lives. In our pursuit of happiness and our need to be productive, having a strong sense of job satisfaction is important. When you are dissatisfied with your job, this can influence your overall outlook on life. Whether you are in a dream job or working your way up the ladder of success, it is always your responsibility to ensure what you are doing satisfies you.

Two of the best things you can do to challenge yourself are to take on more responsibility and get involved in high profile projects. When an organization looks to identify who is next—new supervisors, managers, directors, etc.—one thing they look for is a reasonable and orderly progression in your career and whether or not you have taken on challenging roles in the past. Now, you may not be seeking a management role per se, but any chance you get to indicate that you've increased your responsibilities or taken on challenging tasks or assignments will serve as your advantage factor when compared to your peers.

The Turning Point

Around 2002-2003, I experienced what I call a "Turning Point" in my career. I decided that I was no longer being challenged. At that time, I had been working in Information Technology for about 14 years; I had taken on various assignments within technology. I was very fortunate and, with the help of my mentors and Knowledge Leaders, my early career was both rapid and progressive. I soon reached a point where I grew tired of doing what I had been doing for so many years.

One day, around that time, I walked into my vice president of shared services' office and stated, "I want to do something different, I need a change." Taking on special assignments within the company was always encouraged and, in fact, it was very difficult to achieve senior-level promotions without taking on an assignment outside of your normal day-to-day role. I was 33 at the time, and had been what would be equivalent to a director of IT for a Fortune 500 company. I had been in the same role for 7 years; I felt as though my rapid rise had slowed, and I was bored with what I was doing. The excitement and passion were gone.

My vice president replied, "Mike, we may have some opportunities for you, but it could be anywhere. I will get back to you, but I cannot tell you today what it is or where it will be. Are you still interested?" At that moment, I had to make a split-second decision about my career, my life, and my commitment to the organization as a whole. I knew that, if I said no, I would never get another opportunity and my chances of being promoted would be reduced to no chance at all. The assignment could have been anywhere in the world— my employer was a large global company with a presence in over two hundred countries. I was afraid to just say yes due to the unknown.

Still, I recognized I was the one who had walked into his office and asked for the opportunity. I was also the one bored with my current role. And I was the one who had the need and desire for a new challenge and opportunity to take on more responsibility. As frightened as I was about the unknown, I replied, "Whatever it is, I will do it!" As you can imagine, I walked out of his office a wreck. I kept thinking, *What did I just do?* The assignment could have been in Russia for all I knew. But it was too late now. I had already committed myself. I figured, since I was single and had no immediate family of my own, the risk was worth taking. Since it was just me, I could travel light and move quickly.

My vice president finally got back to me and said, "I have something for you, we need you to represent Shared Services on a top priority project." That project was called Project Angel. Project Angel was an M&A acquisition target project that resulted in a subsequent acquisition in 2005; at the time it was the largest acquisition the company had made.

I was then selected for a few other assignments outside of technology. I was even a lead facilitator at the company's corporate schools program for nearly a year.

Another challenge, which didn't seem that significant back then, was when I was asked by the senior technology leaders to lead a group of board members on a tour of our facilities. Boy was I nervous! I had done a lot of public speaking but not for anyone at that level—they were either CEOs or other high-ranking executives for Fortune 500 companies. Between multiple practice runs—which I hate—I just became more uncomfortable as the day neared. Nonetheless, the day came and I nailed it! I received great feedback from my group of board members. Within my group was our CIO, an executive from HP and John Thompson. You may know Mr. Thompson. He is the former Chairman and CEO of Symantec—a leading security software firm. Today, Mr. Thompson is the chairman of the board of one of the largest technology companies in the world: Microsoft Corporation.

During the three years I was on my 'special assignment' break away from technology, I was consistently challenged and remained outside of my comfort zone—technology. I learned about my strengths and weaknesses and picked up new skills along the way. I quickly realized I had to further develop my business acumen skills and learn a different part of the business. I was also delighted that all of my presentation and public speaking training was put to use. Every assignment was challenging, but I enjoyed every minute of it. I was exposed to new things, new people across the globe, some face time with the most senior managers and board members in the company—I was growing. There was never a dull moment, and the break reinvigorated my passion for technology and how I could further enable the business. It was one of the best decisions I made in my career.

At some time in your career, you will experience a turning point as well—a pivotal moment where you have to make a career defining decision. The odds are, one will certainly be a decision about taking on a new role. When you take on challenging roles, not only does it look good on your resume, it demonstrates your willingness to take on additional responsibility and adapt to change. One key to a progressive career is to continue to care about what you do. You must continue to find what you do interesting, and your passion for that work must remain present.

If you have found you no longer care about what you do, and the passion is no longer burning, find something else to do. Don't be afraid to move outside of your comfort zone. Many people lose the desire and passion for what they are doing, but they let fear and doubt hinder them from making a change.

Throughout your career, you will need to take risks. Don't be overly concerned with having doubts, doubt has never won a fight against confidence. Believe in your ability to kick doubt's butt every time.

Think of every challenging project as a growth meter. You can measure just how much you know and how much more you need to learn at that point in time. If you find yourself on an assignment that is just too easy, it is the wrong assignment for you. Get another one. Remember, the main purpose is to grow with each new project.

Challenges make you discover things about yourself that you never really knew.—**Cicely Tyson**

Differentiate yourself

If you walked into a room full of men with suits with no ties, the suit colors would be different but they would all just be men in suits. Now imagine the same room with the same men, but one or two of them with a colorful pocket square. Who would stand out? You have to be one of the men with the colorful pocket square. That pocket square is your differentiator.

For the context of differentiation, that pocket square represents your exposure to various work assignments, the experience you have gained from them, the skills you developed, the relationships you have built, and the credibility you are building. So, when standing in a room full of your peers, you want to be like the men with the colorful pocket square; you want to stand out. You want to differentiate yourself from the pack. The only way to do that is by doing what your peers are not doing and/or are too afraid to do. While they are comfortable in their current roles, you should be looking to be challenged. When a crisis occurs, and everyone steps back because they are afraid all eyes are on them, you should step forward and lead. You differentiate yourself by daring to be different. You cannot be different if you haven't been challenged.

Offer to help with projects that no one else wants to touch. File the paperwork, lend a hand in getting data input or volunteer to make phone calls. Anytime you take on a new role or project, sitting within each one is an opportunity to grow, which will serve as an investment in your career.

Be willing to commit to the challenge

In this competitive and fast-paced world, if you take a chance and step out of your comfort zone, you may reap rewards that will last a lifetime.

No worthwhile ambition can be accomplished from within your comfort zone. It is only when you give up the security of what is known and take on the discomfort of the unknown that you can grow. As you build your abilities and create new opportunities, you expand the boundaries of your confidence. Your comfort zone increases and you can take on even bigger challenges.

You can never hope to achieve success unless you're willing to embrace change and be committed to challenging yourself. You must also be willing and ready to embrace the discomfort of failure. You must be prepared to get comfortable with the discomfort that comes with taking risks. You do this by continually assessing where you are in your career. Are you letting the fear of failure or the possibility of embarrassment keep you from taking action and moving forward? To make the impact you want to make, ask yourself these questions:

- Am I committed to growing and learning?

- Will I be up for the challenge?

- Am I comfortable with being comfortable?

- Should I accept doing something a certain way just because it has always been done that way?

- Should I seek out new challenges or simply be content with those I already have?

- Do I risk being exposed and vulnerable, or play it safe?

Of course, just because you're willing to take risks and put yourself out there doesn't automatically mean things will all work out. Again, you have to be committed to the challenge, which may involve risk-taking. But, as every successful person will tell you, only by being willing to make mistakes and trying something new will you ever accomplish more than what's been done before. No accomplishment comes with a guarantee of success and never will. Every successful person will tell you they became successful by taking risks—at least a few of them I know. They failed too, but they kept their motivation and objectives intact. They remained committed to growing and learning from their failures and ultimately succeeded.

I can accept failure; everyone fails at something. But I can't accept not trying.—**Michael Jordan**

How well you are challenged will determine who you will become

A decade from now there will no doubt be people who have achieved extraordinary success. One thing is certain—they will not have reached the top by staying safe and within their comfort zone. They will be people who stretched themselves, took risks and continued to challenge themselves. They were willing to take risks and look foolish, knowing the biggest risk is not doing anything. Will you be one of them? In this competitive, fast-paced world, there is very little that comes from playing it safe.

Who you are by the time you reach the end of your AYP years is the person you will be for years to come. If you read Chapter 1 on mentoring, I stated the "core of who you are will be defined between the ages of 22 and 30." So, everything you have experienced, every challenge you have taken on or avoided, and every mistake you have made during those years will shape who you are in the future. It will also shape what you will be doing and, for the most part, how successful you may become. So, challenging yourself today pays off long after your AYP years, after all, you will spend those years shaping the future version of you—what you experience is what you become.

Don't be afraid to fail, you are just growing

In this digital age, filled with 'overnight success' stories, it is easy to overlook the failure and perseverance it took to achieve those dreams.

Failure and determination can be a springboard to much better things. While failing is temporarily painful, it can spur on improvement and growth like nothing else. Trial and error, setback after setback—this is a recipe for greatness and your cue to persist against the odds.

Accept that you will make mistakes along the way, but there is value in the lessons your mistakes teach you. Mistakes are a valuable measure of your progress. If you're not failing from time to time, you may not be challenging yourself and growing.

Accept that the only real failure in this life is not trying to do more.

I've failed over and over and over again in my life, and that is why I succeed.—**Michael Jordan**

It's easy to let mistakes and setbacks define what you can do or who you are. The key is not to focus on the failure itself, but on how you react to it. If you knew that no matter what happens you could handle the outcome, how would that affect the choices you make? What actions would you take that you might otherwise put off?

Now is the time to step up and step out of that box you call the comfort zone. Set your sights on your objectives and face every challenge with a purpose and intent to conquer it. If you do, you will open up the possibility of new opportunities both in your career and in your personal life. Growth and opportunity will always be within reach; you have to decide if you are willing to extend your arms far enough to grab both.

CHAPTER EIGHT

Know the W3H method of working

The times I have been most effective throughout my career have usually been times I had a good handle on what I was managing, who managed all the things I was accountable for, how we would manage everything, and what and when we would measure to check progress and assess our performance. In this chapter, I discuss the What, Who, How and When (W3H) approach and why, if done regularly and effectively, it will help you become a better team contributor, supervisor, manager or executive someday. W3H involves answering the following questions:

- What are you managing?

- Who is responsible for managing it?

- How is it being managed?

- When is it measured?

Don't worry if you don't always get it right. I have been in my field for years, and I still don't get it right every time. But whenever I have, I have achieved the highest of results and, in doing so, developed higher performing teams.

*A particular shot or way of moving the ball can be a player's personal signature, but efficiency of performance is what wins the game for the team. —**Pat Riley***

What are you managing?

One of the most basic things to understand about any role is what the role is, what you are accountable for, and what needs to get done. Whether your occupation is a project manager, attorney, investor or even a janitor, you will have something within the capacity of your role that you are accountable for and that only you can manage. Understanding what you are managing is simply about having a clear understanding of the scope of your responsibilities. For instance, if you are a project manager, your responsibilities will entail managing the projects and its constraints, which include people, cost, and time. An attorney may be accountable for managing the client's case, filing court documents, managing and following up on court inquiries, etc. Everyone, regardless of their occupation, will have a host of things they must manage in order to be effective. To do so, the first thing you must do is know and understand the full scope of what you are accountable for and responsible for managing.

*Either you run the day or the day runs you.—**Jim Rohm***

Who is responsible for what is being managed?

Whenever anyone is accountable for managing the scope of a project, there has to be someone directly responsible for performing the tasks to make sure the job gets done. If you are a single contributor, you may be both accountable and responsible. If you are a supervisor or manager of a team of people, you may have several people responsible for various pieces of the project you are accountable for managing. It's important to understand that accountability and responsibility are distinctly different. You can share your responsibility with others, but you cannot share accountability. Only one person can be accountable. Regardless of the makeup of your team—if you have one, you will ultimately be held accountable for the collective results of all members. If you are a single contributor, accountability and responsibility is pretty obvious.

When you have a team, one tool to ensure clear roles and responsibilities is a Responsible, Accountable, Consulted, and Informed (RACI) chart. I have already talked about the first two items in RACI so let me explain what the latter two mean. When someone is in a consulting role, they have neither accountability nor responsibility, rather they may be sought-after based on their experience in a particular subject. A person who has an informed role contributes nothing to a task or project. Anyone in the informed role is simply notified of what has been decided.

You can use the RACI even if you are a single contributor. If you have several co-workers, you regularly work with on projects, a good way to set clear expectations and understand each other's responsibility in delivering products and services to your customers is by using an RACI chart. It is the most effective way of making individual decisions or collaborating when necessary.

How is what you are accountable for being managed?

Once you have established what you are managing and who is responsible for managing the scope of what you are personally accountable for, you need to put controls in place. Mechanisms and controls are a collection of documents, procedures, processes, and tools used to manage how work will be accomplished. Earlier, I introduced RACI. RACI is actually just one tool you can use to either organize, manage, or govern projects or tasks. Documented procedures, processes, and templates help as well.

If you can't describe what you are doing as a process, you don't know what you're doing.— **W. Edwards Deming**

Some tools to get help in managing what you are accountable for:

- Use RACI charts to outline specific roles and responsibilities

- Document standard procedures for routine, repetitive day-to-day tasks

- Document processes using swim lanes, which are graphical diagrams displayed horizontally or vertically to distinguish responsibility in performing certain tasks or processes. Swim lanes allow you to clearly see your role in the context of the overall process that may intersect several functions across the company

- Identify key metrics that will enable good decision-making

When and what gets measured?

Measurement is the first step that leads to control and eventually to improvement. If you can't measure something, you can't understand it. If you can't understand it, you can't control it. If you can't control it, you can't improve it.—**H. James Harrington**

The saying goes, "You cannot manage what you cannot measure." As cliché as that statement is, it is also absolutely true.

If you have ever been on a few diets, as I have, one of the first things you do is take note of your current state by weighing yourself. This is called your baseline. It is the point at which you start. Then, you set a specified objective to reduce your weight by a certain number of pounds. The number of pounds you want to lose is your objective and your current weight minus the weight you want to lose is your goal. To achieve your objectives and reach your goal, you make adjustments to your eating habits. You may even join a gym or perform other activities all with the hope of achieving your objective and goal. While on your mission to lose weight, you check your weight periodically to see if you have made progress. If not, you will make further adjustments to your diet or increase the exercise regimen to get you on the right track.

A diet, or the entire process of losing weight, is a good example of how measuring for performance and progress works. When you begin to measure, you should always capture a baseline; you can't get to where you're going if you don't know where you've been. Next, you set a target for what you consider to be an acceptable performance level. Once your baseline and target are set, you then devise a plan to get you from your starting point to your target. As you execute your plan, you check your progress regularly using the metrics you identified to see whether or not you have made progress toward hitting your target. If the metrics are trending in the right direction, you know you are doing fine and can stay the course. If no progress is being made or, worse, your performance has somehow fallen below the baseline, you rethink your plan altogether because it is not working.

Having good metrics and measuring the right things help you make more informed decisions. Metrics also drive the right behavior for both you and your team. Measuring what you manage is a large part of what will give you the advantage factor over your peers. Data is always king and the more quantitative measurements you can identify, collect, track, and monitor, the more effective you will be as a professional.

The true measure of the value of any business leader and manager is performance.—**Brian Tracy**

CHAPTER NINE

Know when your time has come

In life, we all will get a chance to say goodbye to something or someone. Often it's difficult, especially when we know it may be for the last time. The same can be said about your current role or your employer. At some point in your career, you will have to say goodbye to the current role you hold within your company and then adapt to a new one—you can't do the same thing forever. Sometimes, you may say goodbye to your current employer altogether and move on to what you may believe are better pastures.

This chapter is about knowing when it is time to make a career change, either horizontally or vertically within your current organization or with an entirely new company. Tough choices, but they are inevitable decisions in a progressive career.

The 'Turning Point'

Some people know when they've reached a point in their career when it is time for a change. Often it is due to their reflection of where they are compared to where they planned to be at that point in time. They usually check their progress against their objectives, formal or informal. If they find they are off track, they make a change—which may be a career defining one.

When you self-reflect and find you are unhappy with where you are in your career, whether it is because you feel you are not growing, not challenged, not moving along fast enough, or you simply feel things can be better,then you have reached your *turning point*. A turning point is a career defining decision that changes your career trajectory. It is a time when you have to face your fears. I can promise you a career change will be one of the scariest things you will ever have to do professionally—no one said getting to where you want to be would be easy!

The fear of change

While fear may prevent you initially from making a career change, ultimately it will be a decision you will have to make, especially if you are an AYP. If you are an AYP, you won't sit still. You will want to grow. Therefore, you will have to move beyond your comfort zone and be challenged. That may mean changing jobs within your current company or taking a new role in another company. No matter what your path, fear will remain constant in your mind throughout. That is natural, but fear should not be an inhibitor to your success.

Why? Because fear can prevent you from realizing your goals. You must decide if you are willing to let fear stop you from achieving your objectives and reaching your goals.

As I mentioned earlier in the book, in 2006 I had to make the most critical decision of my career. Was I afraid? Absolutely! I feared the unknown. I was very comfortable at the time and I knew I would be taking a risk. Just imagine, I had a 17 year career with the same company and I was gainfully employed. To say I feared the unknown would be an understatement; I was scared as hell! Still, no matter how much I feared the unknown, I was more frightened of the thought that I may miss out on promising opportunities elsewhere. I eventually overcame the fear of a new job and a new place and took the risk. To this day, it was one of the best career decisions I have made.

The day will come, if it hasn't already, when you will need to face your fears. You should not worry about being afraid, you will get past that. However, if you are doubtful, you should be concerned. Doubt takes much longer to overcome.

Don't be so quick to run

During your career, always strive to make incremental but progressive steps towards your goals. Outline measurable objectives that will enable you to periodically check your progress toward your goals.

What if you don't realize you're unhappy with your job until someone points it out to you, or you find you are constantly overwhelmed or bored with the tasks you do? This could be a subject that keeps you up at night thinking, *What can I do? What changes do I need to make?* You consult with colleagues, friends and family, in search of an answer. The truth is, you may already know the answer but because it involves a change, and change is hard, you may avoid it. Maybe you simply gripe about it and assume this is why it's called work anyway—it's hard! Often a simple role change within your current company will do the trick. Before you consider leaving a company, think it through thoroughly. Don't be so quick to run. Make sure you have all the answers first and then make a rational decision before ever considering leaving your employer.

Warning signs

I've put together a few signs and red flags that may indicate it is time for you to get out. These are good indicators that your job isn't a good fit anymore, and it's high time to consider making some changes to improve your situation.

- Your company is sinking. If there are valid signs your company is about to go under, you need not go down with the ship. Be sure the signs you are getting are valid before you jump, however.

- You find you lack passion for the work you are doing. You find you are no longer waking up with the same level of excitement and drive you originally felt when you first started. The feeling you had—thinking of all of the opportunities and possibilities—is gone. The truth is, if you're not doing something you love, you may never tap into your full potential. When a job becomes 'just a job', it can be a grind.

- You're stressed out, negative and anxious about work—even when you're not at work. Your work-related stress could even be having a negative impact on your physical health. If the stress is present both at work and at home, it has become all-consuming. Look around and see if your friends and family are affected, too.

- You just don't believe in the company. When you feel there may be ethical or moral differences between you and how your company operates, it can be very uncomfortable. Whatever the issue—be it cultural, ethical, or a difference in how you think the company should operate—you are misaligned with your company, and it may be best to move on.

- Your job performance is suffering. Even if you're up for the task, you find yourself falling behind when getting things done. If you're not productive, consider looking for new work.

- You no longer have a good work-life balance. When you find you're spending less time with your family because of work, or you cannot commit the necessary time to your job, consider looking elsewhere.

- Your skills are not being tapped. You've been passed over for promotion, or your manager doesn't acknowledge your contributions. Maybe you've tried to take on more challenging projects, but those attempts have failed and now you no longer get the high profile tasks. If you feel you have more to offer than what's being asked of you, speak out. If you still feel ignored, you should be looking for new opportunities.

- Your job duties have increased, but the pay hasn't. This is especially true if your company is performing well but it's not reflected in the money you're making or other compensation.

- You really dislike the people you work with. Let's face it, sometimes we can't all just get along. Try to work things out but know that some situations (and some people) just aren't fixable.

- Your ideas are falling on deaf ears. If your ideas are no longer heard or valued or you can't get your manager's attention, think about moving forward and finding a new job.

- You're bored and idling at your job. No matter what you do, it feels like you're stuck in neutral and not growing. If you do the same thing day after day and you're tired of the grind, it's time to stop craving more and get out there!

It's time to change, now what?

Once you realize it might be time to leave your job, you'll want to consider your options. Are you able to walk away without consequence or do you need to search while still working at your current job? Do you want to stay in the same field or explore a career change? What does your ideal job look like? If you would like to, do you have the option of taking a different position within the same company?

Next you'll want to create a game plan for yourself—make lists. Create two to-do lists: one focused on what you need to do to leave your current job and one that centers on the type of job you'd like to have and what you need to do in order to find that next, even better job.

Create an exit strategy

Before you jump ship, you must decide on some key issues such as giving your notice (how much time you will need to continue working), who else you need to tell (always tell your immediate supervisor first so they don't hear it from a little birdie!), and whether or not you'll be needed to train your replacement.

Also, before making that final leap, take the time to compile a 'pros and cons' list so you can get a fresh perspective on your job. Write down what's right with your position and where you've had problems. Make sure you've done all you can to confront the problems you've encountered and be as transparent as you can be. This process will help keep communication open with everyone involved.

And last, but not least, don't let emotions get in the way of your critical decision. It's best to be as objective as possible and make this a purely business decision. Think long and hard before you take the plunge—remind yourself of the compelling reason(s) you've given for making this move. Very importantly, never burn any bridges! You never know when you'll cross paths with a boss or colleague. When you work in the same field, the business world can suddenly become quite small. No doubt you've worked hard to establish a good reputation, so continue to protect that hard work.

In today's fast paced world, the business community is well connected, and technology allows people to talk instantly with one another. Do your best to always be respectful and professional in your endeavors—that might mean taking the high road more often than you'd like.

Sometimes you just have to trust the process; trust you are doing and saying the right thing, even when you can't see it. Have faith in yourself and your capabilities. Remind yourself that your dream job is out there, and you will do whatever it takes to make it your own!

CHAPTER TEN

Always remain focused on your objectives and not the noise

In many work environments, it's easy to get caught up in rumors, small tails, and other noise that in the scheme of things just isn't important. Much of this is unavoidable, but it goes on everywhere. In any workplace, the reality is there will be those who will not like you for reasons unknown and others who will continue to find something wrong in everything you do no matter how great the outcome. Sometimes it will feel like your best is never good enough. Through it all, your job is to simply do your job. Amongst all the chaos and noise, you must continue to remain focused on what you are paid to do—to satisfy your customers and enable your company to grow.

This chapter explores what it takes to focus on the tasks at hand and not on the workplace distractions.

Stay focused

Staying focused really means sticking with your priorities and continuing to reach toward your goal. That means being attentive to your objectives and not getting distracted by all the noise. It also involves executing your plan—taking steps to reach your goals. That's what matters in the end. Know what you are doing and be patient, persistent, and disciplined. Patience will help you overcome the hurdles that will come between you and your objectives, persistence will allow you to come back from inevitable failures, and discipline will allow you to play the game right and resist temptations that could take you off course.

Not everyone will be happy with your decisions

What do you do when you've made decisions that have made others on your team or in your department unhappy? Unfortunately, you can't work on someone else's state of mind. What you can do—deliver inspiration to your colleagues and others on your team. It is up to individual employees to choose to commit and contribute to their own success. Every person is ultimately in charge of his or her own attitude and morale.

It's tempting to spend your time managing and parenting the negative, chronic complainers rather than motivating and leading for success. Don't! Instead, encourage and motivate the efforts of committed employees and handle the naysayers effectively. Concentrate on what you have control over— great quality service, overcoming obstacles, solving problems, and moving forward. The next time you find yourself worrying about the impact a negative attitude can have on delivering your objectives, try a visual exercise: imagine a sports team winning a championship with players bitterly complaining on the sidelines. Would you want to be on that team? What can you do to keep your players happy, cohesive, and moving towards the winning goal?

Good leadership may make people angry

Good leaders are always focused on the well-being of the entire group, not the needs of one or even a couple of people. While providing leadership, you will never make everyone happy; nor should you ever try to—your objective is to be fair and balanced. When you do that, you can be comfortable with your decisions.

Consider the following quote:

Good leadership involves responsibility to the welfare of the group, which means that some people will get angry at your actions and decisions. It's inevitable if you're honorable. Trying to get everyone to like you is a sign of mediocrity: You'll avoid the tough decisions, you'll avoid confronting the people who need to be confronted, and you'll avoid offering differential rewards based on differential performance because some people might get upset. —**Colin Powell**

Mr. Powell, pretty much says it all.

Command is lonely.—**Harry Truman**

Truman is right. Whether you're a CEO or the temporary head of a team project, the buck stops with you. The essence of good leadership is the willingness to make the tough, clear-cut choices that affect the organization as a whole. Even when you strive to create an open and collaborative environment, prepare to be lonely.

Don't focus on what people are saying; focus on what you need to do

Critics and complainers will always whine and complain—no matter how well you lead! Grumblers have a knack for only seeing those few things that don't go well, completely disregarding the many things that do. Constructive criticism is helpful, but the goal of most critics is to challenge your leadership and make things go their way.

Some effective ways to lead well and still put complaints and criticism in perspective

Acknowledge the minority: Face it—unless you are completely incompetent in your leadership, your critics are probably limited to a few people (it may seem like more due to the amount of noise a squeaky wheel can make). They may voice their concerns via emails, texts or social media—using whatever effective technology they can in order to get their point across. The best approach is to acknowledge the complaint and then move on. Don't dwell on the issue once it has been addressed. Don't pay any more attention to it than is initially necessary.

Focus on the majority: The real secret to getting the best of complainers is to ignore them and focus on the concerns of the majority. If you focus all of your decisions and communication on those workers who get things done, the critics have no influence and are effectively silenced.

Divide and conquer: Don't leave this step to last—it can be the most effective card you have to play. If critics are really getting to you, agree to meet with them one on one to discuss any concerns. This will allow them a chance to air their grievances and give you the opportunity to sound them out and exert some influence. Many critics have been won over with focused listening and dialogue. The key is not to react, but to build a bridge. Listen and learn—most importantly, don't compromise your position.

Results will have everyone talking

Results always get a lot of attention because, let's be honest, in business, results are necessary for success. Without results, you can't stay in business! Most organizations have highly effective means of keeping track of who is getting results. In many companies, the emphasis is on results behavior and effective leaders should recognize keys to that action. Results that will have everyone talking begin with a vision. As a leader, you must comprehend what the vision is and be able to share it with your team. You must also have the energy and drive to challenge and motivate people to do their best. Studies show most people value leaders who set, expect, and enforce high standards.

As a leader, you expect your team to behave in a manner consistent with your organization's goals and objectives. By establishing high standards (in conduct, production and results), you set expectations about what behavior and attitude are acceptable. To get the results you want, you also need to provide clear expectations, accountability, decisiveness, and challenging projects.

Leaders must get results to stay in business and be competitive, but they also need to build relationships because people (with their own drives and emotions) do the work. Therefore, both are essential to good leadership. The reality is most leaders are usually good at one and struggle with the other.

Other aspects you can focus on to become a leader who gets results:

- Focus on being strategic—always keep the Big Picture in mind

- Be straightforward in your communications—set clear expectations everyone understands

- Be a good problem solver

- Have a strong focus on tasks

- Be firm but flexible when making decisions and give direction

- Maintain high standards for yourself, as well as others

To create strong results with increased sales, improved customer service, quality, and increased productivity, great leaders must be focused on their objectives and not the noise. They must communicate to make things happen, recognize and accept that not all decisions will sit well with everyone. Leaders focus on what needs to happen instead of what people are saying. The results produced will speak for themselves.

CHAPTER ELEVEN

Exposure and Experience helps you obtain knowledge

Often you want to progress but aren't willing to step into unfamiliar territories to do so. Playing it safe and doing what you know may get you where you want to go, though it will place limitations on how quickly you will grow. Risk-taking and exposure to new things will help you acquire skills to ready yourself for every phrase of your aspiring career. To grow, you have to expose yourself to new things. Once exposed, you must learn that new thing. Mastering something new can take months or even years. When you are exposed and gain experience in something, you acquire knowledge.

Although very brief, this chapter is about how to put yourself in the best position to acquire new skills and grow professionally.

Exposure

They say New York is a city everyone should experience at least once in their lifetime, but just booking a flight to New York and landing there doesn't mean you have experienced New York. It means you were exposed to the city—you know where it is, you know how to get there, and you may even be able to catch a cab downtown.

To experience New York, you have to visit 42nd street, ride the subway system, go to Times Square, maybe even visit Harlem, Greenwich Village or catch a Broadway show. Once you have done a few of those things, you then will have experienced New York versus merely being exposed to it. The same can be said about you professionally. When you are introduced to a new assignment, job function, or skill, you are exposed to something new. Nonetheless, exposure doesn't help you gain experience on that new assignment, within that new department, or in acquiring that new set of skills you will need to succeed. Exposure is only the first step in acquiring knowledge, but it is by far the simplest. Yet you must be exposed to something before you can obtain experience.

Experience

The only source of knowledge is experience.—**Albert Einstein**

While gaining exposure to something new may require little or no action on your part, gaining experience requires your full attention and involvement. Experience is what you acquire through your actions within a certain field or role over time. Again, that can be either a short or long period of time.

You cannot create experience, you must undergo it.—**Albert Camus**

Let's use my earlier example. Once you have gone to Times Square, walked 42nd Street, used the subway, and visited several areas and landmarks, you have experienced New York. You then have acquired enough knowledge to share with others who may be considering a visit to the city. You can then tell them what it feels like, where certain places are, what to look out for, and how best to get around town. By being exposed to New York and experiencing it, you attained knowledge about the city you didn't have prior to visiting. Knowledge is about gaining exposure and then gaining experience.

Experience is work. Experience takes commitment. Experience takes time. Experience will always be your competitive advantage, so try to expose yourself to as much as possible during your AYP years, but also try to gain experience in a diverse group of things. This doesn't mean you need to be all over the map attempting to gain exposure to everything and chasing every experience. It means learn at least 2 to 3 jobs or skill sets within your chosen profession by the time you hit age 30. Many will have been exposed and gained experience in a great deal more, however, you should focus on what *you* can experience.

Nothing ever becomes real till it is experienced.—**John Keats**

Tips on obtaining knowledge within and outside of the workplace:

- Master your current role first

- Take on new assignments and ask for work outside of your comfort zone

- If you move to a new function or take on a different role, align yourself with someone in the department who has a lot of experience

- Be willing to be the 'new guy' several times throughout your career—if it is new to you, you will be the new guy

- Gaining exposure is like a sprint, you can do it fast and with little to no effort, but acquiring experience is a marathon, it will take time

- Doing something for many years doesn't mean you have acquired a lot of experience, you must learn the job, not just be in it—undergo the experience

CHAPTER TWELVE

You don't need a title to be a leader

If you ask several people to define what leadership means, you will get varying descriptions—always! You will also come across people in the workplace, or within your network of associates and friends, who are either in an assigned leadership role or think they are—who believe somehow they have cornered the market on what leadership is or isn't. Trust me, I have met a lot of people like this throughout my career. I promise you will, too.

In this chapter, I discuss my opinion based on my experience of what leadership is or isn't.

Leadership isn't about getting your own way. It's about helping others find theirs—**Nathan Smith**

Leadership boils down to two critical components. First, a leader must have followers. Second, a leader develops other leaders. For me, it is really that simple. I also agree with many others who say leadership is all about influence. Nevertheless, you can gain influence just by being assigned to a leadership role. That alone doesn't necessarily make you a leader. How many people would follow you if you didn't have a formal title or position within an organization? How many people would display the same level of respect for you without a formal title? Think of your current manager, if it weren't for the formal relationship at work, would you follow him/her?

When you can have influence, respect, and support of your team and peers absent an official title, you are a leader.

A leader has followers

Leaders touch a heart before they ask for a hand.—**John C. Maxwell**

No matter how one has obtained their leadership status, leadership must be earned. People must trust your ability to lead and to provide leadership. Only then will they accept you as their leader. When accepted as a leader, you have gained credibility and earned the trust and respect of those around you. When that occurs, others will truly follow you with or without a title; you fulfilled the requirements. For others to follow you, you need not have an *assigned leader* status. *You need no title to be a leader.*

The 'assigned leader'

An assigned leader has been put in a leadership role to lead a small team or larger group of people. Assigned leaders don't always have the necessary leadership skills or ability to lead others, but have somehow been placed in a leadership position. They lead by control, fear, and turning others into order-takers versus guiding individuals to act, think, and grow on their own. In some cases, assigned leaders can be developed into good leaders but not all of them will get there. When someone becomes an assigned leader, but doesn't have the minimum skills to lead others, most likely that person should not have been selected to be a leader in the first place.

Assigned leaders usually have some level of authority because of their position, but they will not yield the same level of influence, credibility, and trust amongst their team members and peers as a *developed leader* will.

A developed leader is someone who has put time and effort into learning how to lead others and has more than likely had a mentor help them develop into a great leader. Always remember, just because someone is placed in a position and authorized to decide for others, it doesn't make them a leader.

What makes a leader?

What makes you a leader is your ability to build relationships, gain credibility, influence, and inspire those on your team to exceed expectations. It is about you helping others recognize their own potential and seeing what is possible. Ultimately, being a leader is about helping others become leaders. When you are doing all of those things without a title, you rock as a leader!

The first phase in becoming a leader is to lead first. You can lead no matter what your occupation or what title you have today, remember, a title isn't necessary to lead or be a leader. You can lead at any time. When you lead early, you will be ahead of yours peers in the race to becoming a great leader.

Lead first to become a leader later

A leader is one who knows the way, goes the way, and shows the way.
—John C. Maxwell

To further understand what makes you a leader, you must first understand the difference between *lead* and *leadership*. When you lead, you show the way. When providing leadership, you know the way and you help others learn what it is. Leaders do both well; they know how to lead and how to provide leadership.

Let's look at this a little bit differently. If you ever used MapQuest, it was always good at showing you the way, but often it included the wrong exits, no information on new construction or traffic challenges, and it always seemed to take longer routes when a shorter one would be available. Often, you used MapQuest's directions until you got to a point where you knew a better way and then you took the route you knew and discarded the MapQuest directions.

On the other hand, if a modern navigation system provides options such as primarily using highways or city streets; avoiding tolls; alternate route if you drive off course; or avoiding traffic jams, it is providing choices that will get you to your destination—you would follow those directions because it not only showed you the way, it actually knows the way and while using it for travel it helps you learn the way. Ultimately, you should strive to be like the navigation system; know the way and teach others how to learn the way. That is leadership. It will take time, but if you are committed to getting there, you will. Before you get there, you must learn to lead before you can provide leadership.

You lead daily and may not know it. When you make a presentation at work, you lead; when you speak within your community, you lead; as a parent, you lead; when you sing solo in your church choir, you lead; and as a teacher you lead your class. In each of these roles, you can influence others and show them the way. When you lead, you can even be effective at getting a lot done through others. Just because you can lead that doesn't mean you are an effective leader or even one who has acceptable leadership abilities. I call these people *taskmasters*. They are very effective at getting a lot done through others, but those whom they lead often learn or grow very little in the process, they are just getting things done! There is nothing wrong being with being a taskmaster. I am one myself and will do it further if necessary. However, like me, you should always strive to have a balance between 'getting it done' and teaching others how to become better workers, team members, and leaders while getting it done.

As a leader, it is no longer all about you. It is about those who look to you for leadership. Learning to lead is a start, but you don't want to stop there. Strive to become a great leader. That takes time and a commitment to continue learning and growing from your experiences—gaining those leader credentials.

When you become a leader, whether at work, within your community or even within a professional organization, you must possess the ability to both influence and inspire others to be great. Like the navigation system, it isn't just about showing the way but explaining and teaching the way. Leadership is about the positive impact you can have on the way others think, live, learn, and grow. Again, you don't need a title to do those things, you just need to obtain the experience, knowledge, and passion to learn and teach others.

A Knowledge Leader can teach you how to be a leader

In Chapter 1, I discussed the concept of Knowledge Leaders. These are the best types of leaders—*someone who has experienced both success and failure while acquiring and developing the necessary knowledge, skills, and know-how to teach others how to lead.* Becoming a Knowledge Leader should be your leadership objective.

If you are an aspiring young professional then you want to be mentored, nurtured, or coached by someone who literally has seen and heard it all. You also want someone who has experienced failure, which is where the best learning takes place. I believe if you haven't learned to fail, you have failed to learn—the student can't be taught if the teacher himself is still learning the lesson.

Find a Knowledge Leader with the credentials and background to help you lead and influence others absent an assigned title. They can tell you what works and what doesn't as well as how to handle challenges along the way. Having a supportive and creditable resource like that in your corner, helping you develop into a great leader, is priceless.

Good leaders develop other leaders

There isn't much to be said about this topic. For me, it's a simple charge for all leaders. If you are a good leader, your duty and responsibility is to pay-it-forward and develop other leaders. Years ago, when I worked at my first company and I taught at their Corporate Schools program, there was one training module: a five minute opening speech based on a quote from one of the founders. The quote was about leaving a legacy. It was not my training module to do initially, but since I loved doing the speech and my peers thought I did it so well, it became my training module to do for every class. I believed in it and it showed. I still live by the basis of that quote which was, "As you progress, be able to look back and identify who you have helped along the way." Ultimately, someone has helped you make it this far.

Simply put, nothing delights me more than seeing my team members at work, mentees outside of work, and others I have worked with as they progress in their careers and become leaders in their own right. That is the kind of legacy the founder was talking about. As a leader, when you develop other leaders you are building your legacy as well. Those leaders will always remember you and you will always remember the feeling.

When you lead, leadership will follow

Leadership doesn't have titles, positions, or external signs. You are a leader once you decide to be. Period. It is a self-fulfilling prophesy. Leadership will never be a role you are given as a promotion—it is something you will strive toward every day, in whatever job you have. To become the leader you dream of and obtain the leadership qualities you seek, to start, you simply must lead. You don't need a title to be a leader, but you must lead before you can provide leadership. When you do both well, you are a leader.

ABOUT THE AUTHOR

Mike A. Williams is an experienced senior information technology executive of Fortune 500 Companies in the financial, insurance and transportation and logistics industries.

A passionate developer and leader of talent, Williams has spent a good part of his career mentoring and advising aspiring young professionals.

A proud native of Paterson, New Jersey, Williams discovered his desire to give back in 1997 when he opened up an Internet Café and began to provide free access to computers for disadvantaged youth. He taught them basic computer and Internet skills. Because of his commitment to community, mentorship, and technology, Williams contributes his time, treasure, and talents to support local and national nonprofit organizations that align with his personal mission and values.

Williams previously served on the boards of the Paterson YMCA, the Greater Paterson OIC, The Urban League of Bergen County, and the National Black Data Processing Associates (BDPA) among others. He was the founder of the Paterson Technology Group, Incorporated (PTGI), a non-profit organization which focused on youth technology and financial literacy skills development. Williams was a founding member and President of Brothers of Paterson Incorporated whose primary mission was to help men within the Paterson, New Jersey community, but quickly became a full community-based organization supporting various community causes.

Williams is a recognized leader within the communities in which he lives and he has been recognized by local, county, and state government officials for his work. He was previously recognized by a former employer and its board of directors for his community work by being the recipient of the Information Services Community Service Award—an award that recognized employees for their service to the communities in which they lived.

Williams is a regular speaker, panelist, and workshop leader on topics covering leadership, technology, and diversity.

A loving father and dedicated mentor, Williams' greatest accomplishments to date are the birth of his daughter and the legacy of leaders he has personally mentored and helped in some way—either to get promoted or move on to the next phase of their career.

Currently residing in Atlanta, GA, Williams loves what he does professionally. He is an active member of BDPA, IT Senior Management Forum (ITSMF), and other associations. He enjoys spending time with his daughter, Mikayla, and actively participating in community-based initiatives locally and back home in Paterson, New Jersey.

Made in the USA
Charleston, SC
18 July 2016